Chikuro Hiroike
1866-1938

Arnold J. Toynbee
1889-1975

Nathaniel Hawthorne
1804-1864

The Civilizational Soul

by

Keisuke Kawakubo

Kojinsha

Copyright © 2015 by Keisuke Kawakubo

All rights reserved. No part of this publication may be reproduced, stored in a retrieval system, or transmitted in any form or by any means, electronic, mechanical, photocopying, recording, or otherwise, without written permission from the publisher.

Published by Kojinsha, Tokyo

ISBN 978-4-905978-90-9

Printed in Japan

Preface

The essays of this collection were presented mainly to meetings of the International Society of Comparative Study of Civilizations (hereafter ISCSC) held at various venues around the world. Editing them has reminded me of the deep debts of gratitude that I owe to many professors, teachers and others, for without their thoughtful comments and suggestions these papers could not have reached their present form. I owe the title of this book to President Andrew Targowski of the ISCSC. In the course of discussing its theme, he said to me, "Keishi [Keisuke], it is a Civilizational Mind." I have changed this phrase, but only slightly, to 'the Civilizational *Soul*.'

There are other particular debts, intellectual and personal, that I must acknowledge. Since my high school days I have been reading and re-reading (at first in Japanese translations) the books of Arnold J. Toynbee. I was given the opportunity to listen to a speech he gave on November 27, 1956, at Tokyo

University where I was a junior at the time, and later had the even greater honor of talking with him at his Oakwood Court home in London on April 26, 1972, when I acted as interpreter for President Sentaro Hiroike of Reitaku University. These blessings impelled me to write a book (in Japanese) on Toynbee, entitled *From Toynbee to Comparative Civilizations* (Kindai Bungeisha, Tokyo, 2000; 646 pages).

Having graduated from the English Department of Tokyo University with a B.A. in 1958, I went on to receive my M.A. from the graduate school of Duke University in 1966, majoring in the study of Nathaniel Hawthorne under the guidance of Professor Arlin Turner. As a result, American literature, and especially Hawthorne, has come to permeate my thinking, and I published (in English) *Nathaniel Hawthorne: His Approach to Reality and Art* (Kaibunsha, Tokyo, 2003; 298 pages) and presented it to Showajoshi University, which awarded me a Litt.D. in 2003 in consequence.

My final debts are more personal still. My parents, Kizo and Kiyoko Kawakubo, initiated me into Moralogy in my younger days, setting me on a path that allowed me to glimpse embodiments of benevolence in Dr. Chikuro Hiroike, the Founder of Moralogy, and my mentor, Dr. Tsuneji Yamamoto, whose blessed presences live still in my memory. My wife, Yasuko Kawakubo has supported me for many years in various ways, and her constant encouragement has made it possible for me to complete the present volume. Lastly I have to acknowledge the continued support of Reitaku University, not least in the publication of this book.

The two lists below represent different arrangements of these essays. The first is chronological, and details the places and the general themes of the meetings at which they were presented. Given the integral concept of the *Civilizational Soul* that this volume is intended to explore, though, I felt it would be more suitable to organize them thematically, hence their rearrangement into the table of contents that appears after the chronological list.

The Essays in Chronological Order

(1) "Hiroike Chikuro and Mori Ōgai as Cultural Initiators in Modern Japan," presented at the 23rd ISCSC meeting, July 9, 1994, at University College, Dublin, Ireland (appears under the modified title of "Two Japanese Masters of the Civilizational Soul: Hiroike Chikuro and Mori Ōgai" in the table of contents).

(2) "Toynbee's View of Religion in an Age of Multi-religious World," presented at the 24th ISCSC meeting, June 15, 1995, at Wright State University, Dayton, Ohio.

(3) "Civilizations and Morals: Legitimacy, the Line of Succession, and Polity," presented at the 25th ISCSC and 50th International World History Association Conference, June 22, 1996, at California State Polytechnic University, Pomona, California.

(4) "Civilization and Religion in Toynbee," presented at the 26th ISCSC meeting, May 8, 1997, at Brigham Young University, Provo, Utah.

(5) "Moralogy (Moral Science): A Meeting of the East and the West," presented at the 27th ISCSC meeting, June 11, 1998, at Reitaku University, Kashiwa, Chiba, Japan.

(6) "The Vistas of the Comparative Study of Civilizations," presented at the 28th ISCSC meeting, May 22, 1999, at St. Louis, Missouri, U.S.A.

(7) "Global Ethics in Practice," presented at the 29th ISCSC meeting, June 8, 2000, at the University of South Alabama, Mobile, Alabama.

(8) "The Status of Japanese Civilization: My Journey for the

Essence of Japan," presented at the 30th ISCSC meeting, June 1, 2001, at Rutgers University, Newark, New Jersey.

(9) "St. Petersburg Viewed from Comparative Study of Civilizations," presented at the 32nd ISCSC meeting, September 18, 2003, in St. Petersburg, Russia.

(10) "Toward Common Wisdom," presented to the 34th ISCSC meeting, June 10, 2005, at the University of St. Thomas, St. Paul, Minnesota.

(11) "The Paths of Spiritual Transmission in the cases of Jesus Christ, Gautama Buddha, and Kūkai," presented to the 35th ISCSC meeting, July 6, 2006, at the Institut Nation d'historie de Art (INHA), Paris, France.

(12) "A Glimpse of China: Past, Present, and Future," presented to the 36th ISCSC meeting, June 14, 2007, at the Asilomar Conference Center, Pacific Grove, Monterey, California.

(13) "America: An Enormous Laboratory of Mankind," presented to the 38th ISCSC meeting, June 27, 2008, at the University of New Brunswick, Saint John, Canada.

(14) "In Search of a New Global Ethics—Toward the End of Hegemony" (*The Bulletin of the Japan Society for Global System and Ethics*, No. 7, 2012).

(15) "The Unprecedentedness of Moralogy Viewed from the History of Western Moral Science" (*Studies in Moralogy*, No. 70, Feb. 2013).

Contents

Preface		iii
Chapter I	The Vistas of the Comparative Study of Civilizations	1
Chapter II	Civilization and Religion	13
Section 1	Civilization and Religion in Toynbee	15
Section 2	Toynbee's View of Religion in a Multi-Religious World	25
Section 3	The Paths of Spiritual Transmission in Case of Jesus Christ, Gautama Buddha, and Kūkai	35
Chapter III	Civilizations and Morals	43
Section 1	Legitimacy, the Line of Succession, and Polity	45
Section 2	Global Ethics in Practice	55
Section 3	Toward Common Wisdom	65
Chapter IV	Two Civilizations and One City	81
Section 1	My Journey in Search of the Essence of Japanese Civilization	83
Section 2	America: "An Enormous Laboratory" of Mankind	91
Section 3	A Glimpse of China: Past, Present, and Future	101
Section 4	St. Petersburg Viewed from Comparative Civilizations	109
Chapter V	The Civilizational Soul	119
Section 1	Introducing Moralogy: Bridging the East and the West	123
Section 2	For the Internationalization of Moralogy A Tentative Reply to Dr. Lauwerys' Proposals on National Ortholinon	135
Section 3	Two Japanese Masters of the Civilizational Soul: Hiroike Chikuro and Mori Ōgai	155
Section 4	The Unprecedentedness of Moralogy Viewed from the History of Western Moral Science	169

Notes 187
Bibliography 209
Index 217

About the Author
Keisuke Kawakubo was born in Kochi City, Japan, in Sept. 1935. Graduated from the English Department, Tokyo University, B.A. (1958), and Duke University, M.A. (1966), and received a Litt.D. from Showajoshi University in 2004. Chairman (1990–1996) of the English Department, Dean (1996–2000) of the College of Foreign Languages of Reitaku University; President (2001–2003) of the Nathaniel Hawthorne Society of Japan, life member of the Nathaniel Hawthorne Society of America since 1978, and Vice-President (1998–) of the International Society for the Comparative Society of Civilizations, which Arnold J. Toynbee and Pitirim Sorokin founded in Saltsburg, Austria. His major works are *From Toynbee to Comparative Civilizations* (2000), 646 pp. in Japanese and *Nathaniel Hawthorne: His Approach to Reality and Art* (2003), 298 pp. in English and this book, *The Civilizational Soul* (2015). He is Professor Emeritus and Visiting Professor of the Center for the Comparative Study of Civilizations and Cultures, Reitaku University.

Chapter I

The Vistas of the Comparative Study of Civilizations

Chapter I

The Vistas of the Comparative Study of Civilizations

I

It is a good time for us now, in the Janus years A.D. 1999 and 2000,* to reflect on some theoretical possibilities of the comparative study of civilizations by analyzing distinguished achievements of preceding scholars and by exploring future possibilities in this field of study.

There may be various approaches to the comparative study of civilizations. Each has some meaning if it has the comparative point of view and if it studies a number of aspects of civilizations. In my case I first studied Arnold Toynbee in his life and work; then I gradually extended (or expanded) my field of study to other civilizationists. I stand now on the *Janus* ground: what the comparative study of civilizations was, is, and could be.

Herman Melville, the author of *Moby-Dick*, displayed a penetrating insight about the nature of America in his autobiographical novel, *Redburn* (1849), as follows:

For who was our father and our mother? Or can we point to any Romulus and Remus for our founders? Our ancestry is lost in the universal paternity; and Caesar and Alfred, St. Paul and Luther, and Homer and Shakspeare [sic] are as much ours as Washington, who is as much the world's as our own. We are the heirs of all time, and with all nations we divide our inheritance.[1]

As its later history proves true, America presents a rich soil for the growing comparative study of civilizations. Since the seeds and saplings of comparative civilizations were transplanted from European soil to America in the beginning of the 1970s, a series of intellectual giants such as Sorokin (integralism and altruism), Alfred Kroeber (comparison becomes possible by adding the concept of style to Toynbee's civilizational change), Bagby (peripheral civilizations), Quigley (scientific methodology with clarity), McNeill (world history), Melko (whole nature of comparative civilizations), Palencia-Roth (comparative literature with fresh idea of cartography), Wescott (encyclopaedic knowledge based on linguistics), Wilkinson (Central Civilization), debate between civilizationists and world systemists in *Comparative Civilizations Review*, No. 30 and Sanderson, ed., *Civilizations and World Systems*,[2] and many other distinguished scholars made their contributions.

On the other hand, Japan has been a unique place into which aspects of both Eastern and Western civilizations have been flowing, and has Japanized them in her rich soil. Since the Meiji Restoration, we have had a series of distinguished civilizationists such as Yukichi Fukuzawa (the civilizationist in modern Japan), Tadao Umesao (ecological view of civilizations), Shin Yamamoto (peripheral civilizations), Shuntaro Ito (six stages of civilizations based on erudition of the East and the West),

Masahiko Kamikawa (a turning point of the axis of co-ordinates in the history of methodology) and many others. Is there any room left for further development of the comparative study of civilizations? My presentation is a modest but sincere possible answer to this question.

II

The comparative study of civilizations in itself implies a global perspective, covering the present, past, and future. It is something like a great sea into which many rivers of thought, philosophy, religion, language and culture flow for many years and even centuries, ever widening and increasing in volume. Since the establishment of ISCSC in 1961, mainly a river of researches by great Western scholars has been flowing in. Last year we had for the first time the "Dialogue between ISCSC and JSCSC"[3] at Reitaku University in Japan, but it was just a beginning. There must have been many works of civilizationists in a broad sense in various countries and civilizations, done separately, independently, and unknown to each other because of time, space and language barriers.

In this ISCSC there have been mostly the works of Western scholars discussed; it seems to me, therefore, that there may be some neglected areas or civilizations, particular emphases, biases, and even blind points. Our past president Michael Palencia-Roth[4] enriches our view of civilizations by mentioning often neglected names and learning in Latin America. In this context, it is laudable that some civilizationists and world system theorists such as David Wilkinson,[5] William McNeill,[6] and Andre Gunder Frank[7] have attempted to restore an imbalanced view of world history based on Eurocentrism to a more well-balanced view. But they are exceptional. I presume that the main causes are the lack of available Eastern sources and the language barrier for Western scholars.

Professor Eckhardt points out that the available sources for Western civilizationists are inevitably Eurocentric, for example, he writes:

> Sorokin (1937–41, Vol. 4, pp. 328–29) also provided a measure of cultural values going back to 4000 B.C., but the data were rather sketchy until the 11th century B.C., and they were more Eurocentric than Kroeber's geniuses, since Europeans constituted 85 percent of the total. These data represented historical persons who were mentioned in the 9th edition of the *Encyclopedia Britannica*, which was published in 1875–89, as having made a notable contribution to one or more fields of culture, including statesmanship, philosophy, religion, literature, fine arts, miscellaneous scholarship, science, music, and business.[8]

Needless to say that Sorokin is a great scholar, but perhaps if he had used a different encyclopaedia in different civilizations, he might have seen a different picture of the world civilizations.

Scholars build their theories based on their available sources. If their sources are imbalanced, their theories based on such sources must also inevitably be imbalanced. Western scholars have advantages and disadvantages in sources as well as Eastern scholars. For the past century, both Eastern and Western scholars have applied Western theories for the interpretation of things Eastern. In the field of natural sciences, say, in the principle of electricity, it can work universally. But in the field of social sciences and humanities, theories based on Western sources are not always applicable to things Eastern.

I will give one example. Most Japanese archaeologists

have been spellbound by "the Neolithic Revolution" of Gordon V. Childe (1892–1957), who maintains that wheat agriculture started about 10,000 years ago in Mesopotamia, while rice agriculture was hitherto believed to have begun 3,000 years later in the East. Because agriculture is the momentum for civilizations, his theory led us to the lineal and Eurocentric view of civilization from Mesopotamia—Egypt, Greece and Rome and then medieval Europe and modern West, and inevitably supported modern European world dominance. Recently, however, many discoveries have been made about the origin of rice agriculture. For example, Professor Yan Wenming[9] of Beijing University, using C14 dating, discovered that rice agriculture started 15,000–14,000 years ago along the middle and the lower reaches of Chang Jiang River in China and also reported that earthenware of 15,000 years ago was discovered. A Japanese scholar Takashi Tsutsumi[10] writes that earthenware of 16,000 years ago was uncovered at Shimomouchi, Nagano prefecture, Japan. Professor Yoshinori Yasuda maintains that the theory based on the West Wheat Crescent cannot apply uncritically to the interpretation of the whole history of mankind.[11]

III

To make a better balance, let me introduce two Japanese comparativists, the one is Kūkai（空海）or Kōbō-Daishi（弘法大師）(774–835), the other is Jiun Sonja（慈雲尊者）(1718–1804). Kūkai, founder of Shingon Sect of Buddhism, is considered to be the first man who formulated a systematic comparative thought in his *Sangō Shīki*, 3 volumes (797),[12] which is a comparative study of Buddhism, Confucianism, and Taoism in the form of a drama, and *Himitsu Mandala Jūjūshinron*, 10 volumes (c. 830),[13] which is a comparative study of various religions and philosophical thoughts in India, China, and Japan, and a detailed exploration of ten stages of religious and moral minds. Kūkai's Esoteric Buddhism is sometimes associated with magical powers, incantations, lighting a holy fire for invocation, and it is believed that he has been living in meditation in Mt. Kōya and will be waiting for the coming of Maitreya Bodhisattva 5.67 billion years in future.[14]

He seems to be very mystical. But when the esoteric mist is cleared away from Kūkai, his figure appears more realistic to us, though still great. He worked very hard for the betterment of people by building bridges, digging wells, making ponds for agriculture, and founding the first private university in Japan. His style is superb. If you read the above mentioned *Sangō Shiki*, for example, you will find it sparkling with gems of the classical works of Confucianism, Taoism and Buddhism. If we have some amount of classical knowledge, it is not impossible to understand it, because its style is very clear, and full of familiar names, phrases, and events in the classical world. It is even modern, in the sense of the modernist writings of Ezra Pound and T. S. Eliot. We can share a common classical heritage with Kūkai. He is the first systematic comparatist in Japan.

Before Western science and technology were brought into Japan, learning in Japan was required to combine intellectual pursuit and one's own moral perfection. Jiun was exemplar in this goal: a great scholar with fine character. Though at the age of 41 he retired to the secluded place of Mt. Ikoma, this philologist's eye was open to the world, reading world maps and was interested in Mongolia, Manchuria, China, India, Holland, London, Paris, Napoleon, the Copernican theory, amongst others, and once in a while he went down to, then in his later years lived in, Kyoto to give lectures on Buddhism and

Shintoism and had a great moral influence on many people. He did not stop writing until the age of 85 nor stopped lecturing until the time of his death at the age of 87. He left over one thousand and several hundred volumes in Japanese bookbinding, only about 300 volumes of which were published in Western bookbinding from 1921 to 1935.[15]

Though Jiun belonged to Kūkai's Shingon Sect, he had no interest in things magical. He was conspicuous in his scientific attitude toward truth, disregarding the differences among sects or religions[16] and devoted himself to education on how to become a true human being.[17]

IV

At the very end of the 20th century, even natural scientists are strongly required to have moral spirit. Why shouldn't we incorporate moral value in the theories of comparative study of civilizations? Sorokin was criticized because he includes value in his system. "Because the modern academy has relegated transcendentals to philosophy and theology, it has not been feasible to constitute a scientific self within such a framework."[18] But Sorokin has his Integralism which is the foundation of his system of social thought.[19] As Vincent Jeffries writes:

> Sorokin's idea of integralism was derived from his historical study of culture types and their systems of truth and knowledge (Ford, 1963). Three types of integrated culture were described: Ideational, Sensate, Idealistic. The system of truth and knowledge is the compartment of culture which pertains to ontology and epistemology.[20]

Jeffries maintains that "the problem of incorporating the

truth of faith in the contemporary social sciences has been considered in some detail in a previous paper." (Jeffries, 1999. See also Jeffries, 1997.)[21]

Toynbee was also criticized because of his metahistory. But "he meant by History a vision—dim and partial, yet (he believed) true to reality as far as it went—of God revealing Himself in action to souls that were sincerely seeking Him."[22]

The concluding part of "The Historian's Angle of Vision" is as follows:

> History's contribution is to give us a vision of God's creative activity on the move in a frame which, in our human experience of it, displays six dimensions. The historical angle of vision shows us the physical cosmos moving centrifugally in a four-dimensional frame of Space-Time; it shows us Life on our own planet moving evolutionarily in a five-dimensional frame of Life-Time-Space; and it shows us human souls, raised to a sixth dimension by the gift of the Spirit, moving, through a fateful exercise of their spiritual freedom, either towards their Creator or away from Him.[23]

If history should have a holistic view, we can say that the above is quite valid.

V

Samuel P. Huntington's "Clash of Civilizations?" in *Foreign Affairs* (Summer 1993) and his revised and enlarged book, *The Clash of Civilizations and the Remaking of World Order* (1996) had a sensational impact. Many people, probably influenced by the *Foreign Affairs* article, criticized part of the title, *The Clash of Civilizations*, and condemned him for not saying the "symbiosis" of civilizations. Few have discussed squarely the latter half of the book title, *the Remaking of World Order*. In actual fact Huntington discusses the symbiosis of civilizations, and writes as follows:

> Instead of promoting the supposedly universal features of one civilization, the requisites for cultural coexistence demand a search for what is common to most civilizations. In a multicivilizational world, the constructive course is to renounce universalism, accept diversity, and seek commonalities.[24]

He proposes three rules on how to avoid the clash of civilizations:

> At least at a basic "thin" morality level, some commonalities exist between Asia and the West. In addition, as many have pointed out, whatever the degree to which they divided humankind, the world's major religions—Western Christianity, Orthodoxy, Hinduism, Buddhism, Islam, Confucianism, Taoism, Judaism—also share key values in common. If humans are ever to develop a universal civilization, it will emerge gradually through the exploration and expansion of these commonalities. Thus in addition to the abstention rule, and the joint mediation rule, the rule for peace in a multicivilizational worlds is the commonalities rule: peoples in all civilizations should search for and attempt to expand the values, institutions, and practices they have in common with peoples of other civilizations.
>
> This effort would contribute not only to limiting the clash of civilizations but also to strengthening Civilization in the singular (hereafter capitalized for clarity). The singular Civilization presumably refers to a complex mix of higher

levels of morality, religion, learning, art, philosophy, technology, material well-being, and probably other things.[25]

Civilizationists and moral scientists are experts at finding commonalities of world religions. If the comparative study of civilizations is one of the mission-oriented sciences like peace studies, why do we not explore the commonalities?

In conclusion, my proposal is as follows:

1. To make a holistic "comparative study of civilizations," we have to gather more balanced sources and perspectives covering the East and the West and the North and the South. This statement, however, does not necessarily exclude and devalue particular studies based on particular sources.
2. Since civilizations include culture, which contains religion, philosophy, morality, *Weltanschauung* and others related with value, the comparative study of civilizations has room to incorporate value in it.
3. An aspect of the comparative study of civilizations is that it is a mission-oriented science: to decrease human misery, folly, greed and arrogance, and to increase human happiness and welfare, and to elevate the levels of truth, goodness, and beauty among humankind.

Chapter II

Civilization and Religion

Chapter II

Civilization and Religion

Section 1

Civilization and Religion in Toynbee

I. A brief sketch of the development of Toynbee's view of history

Arnold J. Toynbee's view of history metamorphosed itself during his long lifetime. The stage of development began with a study of national history conveyed to him in his childhood by his mother. The second was a study of civilization as "an intelligible field of historical study." (*A Study of History*, Vols. I–VI) At this stage his view of history was cyclical: birth, growth, breakdown, and disintegration of civilizations. In the phase of disintegration, schism of the soul occurs; the civilization contains the universal state by dominant minority and the universal church by an internal proletariat, and an external proletariat (barbarian) out of the limes of a civilization. Thirdly the failure of the concept of civilization as an intelligible field of historical study led to a new idea which came in the transient period of his writing volumes VI and VII. Now, higher religion was more important than civilization from the standpoint of transrationalism. He meant by history "a vision...of God revealing Himself in action to souls that were sincerely seeking Him." (X, 1)[1]   The goal of history was the Kingdom of God. Thus his view of history changed from a cyclical theory to a progressive one.

II. The relation of higher religions to civilizations

At first we have to understand the relation between higher religions and churches in Toynbee's usage of the terms:

> [T]he churches are embodiments of the higher religions, and are diverse approximate projections on Earth of one and the same *Civitas Dei*, and [are] of a spiritually higher order than the species represented by the civilizations. (cf. VII, 526)

More precisely, in his *Study of History, Illustrated* (1972), he writes as follows:

> Churches are the institutional embodiment of higher religions, and the true mission of higher religions, which distinguishes them from religions of earlier kinds, is to enable human beings to enter into a direct personal relations with a trans-human presence in and behind and beyond the Universe. (*Illust*. p. 333)[2]

We have discussed the relation of churches to civilizations, and we have concluded that churches are a distinctive species of societies [in his *Study*, VII (1954), "Churches as a Higher Species of Societies"] that cannot be made intelligible if they are treated, not as being institutions of a new kind, but as being simply the religious facets of the culture of the civilizations within which they have arisen.... Churches, we have found, break out of the frameworks of civilizations, and this is why churches need to be treated as being societies of a separate and distinctive kind. (*Illust.* p. 343)

Toynbee examines three conceptions of the relationship between civilization and religion. First, religions are cancerous; second, religions play the role of chrysalises for a creation of a new civilization; third, churches are higher species of societies.

a. **Churches as Cancers**

Are the higher religions anti-social and harmful to civilizations? Toynbee writes as follows:

> When there is a shift in the focus of human interest and energy from the ideals aimed at in the civilizations to those aimed at in the higher religions, is it true that social values, for which the civilizations claim to stand, are bound to suffer?.... Is the fabric of civilization undermined if the salvation of the individual soul is taken as being the supreme aim of life? (VII, 386)

When we look at the decline and fall of the Roman Empire and the contemporary rise of Christianity, we are inclined to think that the religion is a social cancer to the civilization. James Frazer maintains this view toward Christianity in contrast with Greek and Roman ethics:

> Greek and Roman society was built on the conception of the subordination of the individual to the community, of the citizen to the state; it set the safety of the

commonwealth, as the supreme aim of conduct, above the safety of the individual whether in this world or in a world to come.... All this was changed by the spread of Oriental religions which inculcated the communion of the soul with God and its eternal salvation as the only objects worth living for, objects in comparison with which the prosperity and even the existence of the state sank into insignificance.... The earthly city seemed poor and contemptible to men whose eyes beheld the City of God coming in the clouds of heaven. (Quoted in VII, 384)

The Graeco-Roman world—the far-shining cities and stately porticoes, in the art, politics and science of Antiquity—had descended into the great hollow which is roughly called the Middle Ages, extending from the fifth to the fifteenth century. J. C. Morison, *The Service of Man: an Essay towards the Religion of the Future.* London, 1887, Kegan Paul, Trench, pp. 177-78, summarized by me. (VII, 383)

Because of the abandonment of the traditional worship of the Hellenic pantheon by pagan converts to Christianity and the suppression of Paganism by the Christian Emperor Theodosius, the Roman Empire was supposed to decline and fall. Saint Augustine wrote his *De Civitate Dei* in order to answer to this pagan thesis. (*A Study of History,* X, 87-91)

b. Churches as chrysalises

This view reflects that churches are useful "in keeping the species of society known as civilizations alive by preserving a precious germ of life through the perilous interregnum between the dissolution of one mortal representative of the species and the genesis of another." (VII, 392) Toynbee admits that this view is partially true. (VII, 393 and "The Inadequacy of the

Chrysalis Concept," 410–419) Toynbee concludes: "Chrysalis churches were evidently not a necessity of life for the species of society known as civilizations; and this observation suggested that, conversely, the species of society known as churches could not have come into existence simply in order to perform this service." (VII, 419)

c. **Churches as a higher species of societies** (VII, 420–525)[3)]
Toynbee's classification of societies is as follows:

4. Higher Religions.
3. Secondary Civilizations.
2. Primary Civilizations.
1. Primitive Societies. (VII, 448)

The above serial order is "not only chronological and genealogical but is also qualitative.... [T]he order reveals itself as an ascending scale of values in four degrees." (VII, 448) Generally and by definition, the comparative study of civilizations does not deal with 1. "Primitive Societies." Toynbee puts higher religions into a category separate from civilizations. His term, "universal churches," means the embodiment of higher religions, though any earthly manifestation has limitations and defects, for example, the Christian church in the Roman Empire. In the above classification, No. 4 "Higher Religions" should be considered as universal churches, because the former sounds more abstract and not suitable for the name of a species of society. Nevertheless, Toynbee set up "a higher species of society" than civilizations, and he discussed at length the nature of that society (VII, 420–569). He mentions Saint Augustine's *Civitas Dei*, the Kingdom of God, in connection with his "higher species of societies."

Where are they? If the *Civitas Dei* is in Heaven, not on earth, it is not an object of history but of theology. Since the universal churches are an embodiment of higher religions, they must be in this world, not in heaven. The universal churches could be, therefore, the object of historical studies.

d. Toynbee's concept of "a higher species of society" and Saint Augustine's *Civitas Dei* [4]

Saint Augustine (354–430) wrote his *De Civitate Dei* (413–26) during the decline of the Roman Empire. Toynbee discusses Saint Augustine's concept of relations between the mundane and the supra-mundane commonwealth, saying that "Saint Augustine takes Love as his touchstone." (VI, 365)

Saint Augustine writes: "The great distinction which differentiates the two commonwealths—the society of the religious and the society of the irreligious—is this: in the one the love of God comes first, in the other the love of Self." (*De Civitate Dei*, Book XIV, chap. 13. Quoted in Toynbee's *Study*, VI, 364) The two commonwealths are, therefore, different in quality or kind. Toynbee's concept of "a higher species of society" and civilizations roughly corresponds to Saint Augustine's *Civitas Dei* and the irreligious respectively.

Toynbee raises another question, i.e. "the attitude which the citizen of the supra-mundane commonwealth ought to take up, in his pilgrimage through This World, towards the institutions of the mundane commonwealth which he will find in force around him." (VI, 366) He summarizes Saint Augustine's view as follows: it is the duty of the pilgrim-citizen of the supra-mundane commonwealth to avoid the snares of This World and it is legitimately allowed for the pilgrim-citizen to make of the institutions of the mundane commonwealth as a matter of practical convenience. (VI, 368) So long as the manners and customs of This World are not against those of the supermundane, the pilgrim-citizens are expected to follow them. They are "citizens of This World and of the *Civitas Dei* simultaneously." (VII, 559)

Toynbee examines the contents of the Church or a higher species of society, painfully, in a sense, because he is well aware that the Church is not the perfect manifestation of the kingdom of God. It is, however, the "Bow of the Cloud." (VII, 551–568, Exodus 9: 12–17)[5]

III. Toynbee's methodology and epistemology

What is the object of history? If it is the description and analysis of apparent "facts" in a specific space and time, then Toynbee in his later years could not be an historian. He was bitterly criticized by many "historians" after the publication of *A Study of History*, Vols. VII–X, 1954. In fact, he endured hundreds of arrows of criticism and published volume XII, *Reconsiderations* in 1961, which is one of the most perfect models of scholarly conscience. We are now entering the realm of methodology and epistemology.

The object of his history is as follows:

> History's contribution is to give us a vision of God's creative activity on the move in a frame which, in our human experience of it, displays six dimensions. The historical angle of vision shows us the physical cosmos moving centrifugally in a four-dimensional frame of Space-Time; it shows us Life on our own planet moving evolutionarily in a five-dimensional frame of Life-Time-Space; and it shows us human souls, raised to a sixth dimension by the gift of the Spirit, moving, through a fateful exercise of their spiritual freedom, either towards

their Creator or away from Him. (X, 2)

What a grand view of history! And this grand view of history invited many historians' anger. British and other Western historians felt that Toynbee had no love and sympathy toward his own country, and Western civilization in general. They denounced Toynbee for misunderstanding and distorting several facts. Pieter Geyl writes as follows:

> The real truth of the matter is, of course, that there is an incompatibility between Toynbee's mental attitude towards the past and that of "the historians." They would not care if he wrote as a prophet, but they feel that the best traditions of their profession are insulted when the prophet poses as a historian.[6]

I think this is an example of the differences of definitions of historians and history. If you take traditional and limited definitions, Geyl is right. Obviously Toynbee deviated from the traditional realm of historians. But I think that this differentiation is a positive point. No ordinary historian could differentiate on such a grand scale as Toynbee.

Toynbee in his later years adopted a trans-rationalist attitude, which is connected to his later view of history. "The Issue between Trans-rationalists and Rationalists" (XII, 68–80) is important. Toynbee expounds as follows:

> I think that an inquirer who holds, as I myself hold, that rationalism is not enough ought, none the less, to follow the rationalists' good example of recognizing that the human reason's mental net is binding in so far as it is truly effective in apprehending Reality.... At the same time I am

alive to the limitations of human reasoning power, and I am convinced that there are questions which reasoning cannot answer but which human beings are nevertheless bound to ask, because one would be less than human if one did not ask them and did not go on to try to answer them, even though one's answers to such 'trans-rational' questions will be, by definition, unverifiable.... From this 'transrational' point of view, Reality looks like a house of many mansions, and our human reason's mansion does not seem to be self-contained, or, indeed, even semi-detached. (XII, 74–75)[7]

IV. The Role of religion in the 21st century

Finally, I would like to mention the future role of religion. On many parts of the earth, we now have a secularized and mechanized society. Some are highly industrialized societies in which human aspiration to seek the transcendental and spiritual is often suppressed. When this desire becomes distorted, we have Aum Shinrikyou which attacked people with the salin gas on the Tokyo subway; 39 members of Heaven's Gate cult who committed suicide. In 1978, at the Peoples Temple in Jonestown, more than 900 cult members also committed suicide because their leader, Jim Jones, decided it was time. These are but a few examples of religious fanaticism. When a certain religion or a sect believes that it is best and absolute, while all others are evil, then religious wars occur. We can hardly approve this kind of religions. When people believe only a transcendental value and despise earthly things, this happens. True religions must pursue bringing the Kingdom of God to Earth. Religions must learn the lessons of history and the results of modern science, and contribute to the welfare of mankind. Toynbee's view of religions is well-balanced and worth-while.[8]

Chapter II

Civilization and Religion

Section 2

Toynbee's View of Religion in
a Multi-Religious World

I

After the September 11, 2001 attacks on the World Trade Center in New York City and the Pentagon in Washington D.C., both of which are the sanctuaries of money and power, the world has been pressed to be enlightened on the matter of religion. The problem of religion is one of the imperative issues as to how mankind can live together in a peaceful coexistence.

I would like to discuss the desirable attitude of mankind toward religions and also civilizations by referring to Toynbee's view of religion. If I may partly use Professor Samuel P. Huntington's controversial article, "The Clash of Civilizations?" and his book, *The Clash of Civilizations and the Remaking of World Order*,[1] we must say that mankind should not have "the clash of religions and civilizations" from now on.

Present circumstances around religions of the world are totally different from those of ancient, medieval, and early modern times because of the advance of science and technology such as methods of communication and transportation, and the globalization of the economy, politics, and culture. In former days, the spacial boundaries of an individual's known world were very limited. In such circumstances, people could be content with their limited faith. When one religion tried to enforce its religion into another religious area, religious conflicts occurred.

Some aggressive religions tend to demand as follows: "Our religion is the best, and your religion is inferior and wrong." This tendency is strong among missionary religions.[2] The more earnest and faithful they are, the fiercer the religious conflicts become, and in the extreme cases, religious wars occurred in the past. These are very lamentable phenomena and they are not consistent with the will of the founders of the religions. Faithfulness is praiseworthy; however, when it goes with narrow-mindedness, the result is deplorable.

Let me introduce here a tale by Nathaniel Hawthorne. He wrote many tales of Puritans in New England, one of which is "The Man of Adamant."[3] Richard Digby, the hero, fancies himself uniquely chosen for salvation. He leaves his village and walks into the forest until he finds a cave. He says, "Here I can read the Scriptures, and be no more provoked with lying interpretations."[4] Mary Goffe—in reality only a spirit—came from England to rescue Richard. He says, "Perverse woman!... I tell thee that the path to Heaven leadeth straight through this narrow portal, where I sit. So saying, he opened his Bible again, and fixed his eyes intently on the page."[5] Hawthorne put an ironical comment on it. "The shadow had now grown so deep, where he was sitting, that he made continual mistakes in what he read, converting all that was gracious and merciful, to denunciations of vengeance and unutterable woe, on every created being but himself."[6] He died in the cave, and more than a century later, he was discovered *petrified* in the cave by some children playing in the area of Digby's cave.   Of course this is fiction.   Fiction, however, can sometimes tell more truth, as Aristotle says in his *Poetics*[7] than facts.   Though this tale is an extreme case, it tells us very vividly about the stupidity of bigotry and fanaticism.

II

In an Age of Ecumenism
The term, "ecumenism" is often used to mean the universality of Christianity; however, I mean here the tendency and necessity to seek the common nature of not only Christianity but also all other religions and cultures of the world.   It does not mean, however, nor expect the coming of one monolithic religion and culture in the world.   It means recognizing the unique merit of each belief; figuratively speaking, to let each play a part in a symphony and, as a whole, have a global symphony orchestra.

The diversity of higher religions and difficulty to be free from bias
We have to recognize the diversity of higher religions.   The reason why we believe in a particular religion is mostly historical accident: we are destined to be born and brought up in a particular time and place.   Very few could choose a particular religion as his or her own faith after deliberate and comprehensive research on many higher religions in the world. Toynbee is an exceptional man: he tried to be fair[8] to many religions and to transcend his particular historical background. He, however, confesses as follows:

The personal *tour de force* which an historian has to attempt if he is to perform his professional service for his fellow human beings is to correct, by imagination, the bias inherent in the standpoint at which he has been placed by the historical accidents of his birth and upbringing, in order to see and present the flux of human life *sub specie aeternitatis*. But human attempts to see human affairs through God's eyes must always fall infinitely short of success; and, while it is difficult enough for the historian to correct his political bias as a citizen of a state and his cultural bias as a member of a society, the hardest of all the feats of imagination that are required of him is to see beyond the *Weltanschauung* of an ancestral higher religion....[9]

The diversity of higher religions as reflections of diversity of Jungian psychological types

God or the Ultimate Spiritual Reality is infinite and transcends all our human understanding. In order to understand It, It must be reflected through a particular time and place, a particular language and culture, a particular eye and the vision of a particular human being. When a man catches God or Ultimate Spiritual Reality, it is only a part of it, not all of it.

Toynbee interprets the existence of various higher religions through Jung's psychological types.[10] Winetrout aptly summarizes:

> We add Jung to Toynbee, and lo and behold we arrive at a synthesis of higher religions and human personality types [the introvert and the extrovert plus four human functions: thinking, feeling, sensation, and intuition].... The patterning becomes very neat. Two religions are Indic in origin: Hinduism and Buddhism. These two are the

introvert pair with Hinduism displaying the thinking bias and Buddhism the intuitive bias. Two religions are Judaic in origin: Christianity and Islam. These two are the extrovert pair with Christianity indicating a love bias and Islam a sensation bias.[11]

The above statement, therefore, implies: Claiming to possess a monopoly of the Divine Light is *hubris*.
Toynbee writes as follows:

> If the writer were to be asked: 'Do you believe or disbelieve that Christianity or any other higher religion is an exclusive and definitive revelation of Spiritual Truth?' his answer would be: 'I do not believe this. I believe that any such claim is an error which is at the same time a sin. In claiming to possess a monopoly of the Divine Light, a church seems to me to be guilty of hybris. In denying that other religions may be God's chosen and sufficient channels for revealing Himself to some human souls, it seems to me to be guilty of blasphemy.[12]

Toynbee's standpoint as a Symmachan

Toynbee mentions the name of Quintus Aurelius Symmachus (c. 345–c. 405), whenever he needs to explain his personal religious view and his attitude toward higher religions in general. Symmachus was a Roman government official and orator, who argued for the retention of the old Roman religion in official state functions, but was successfully opposed by St. Ambrose (340?–397). Toynbee writes as follows:

> I am not entitled to call myself a Christian; I must call myself a Symmachan. Symmachus's confession of faith— "The heart of so great a mystery can never be reached by

following one road only"—is an article in my creed which neither my head nor my heart will allow me to abandon.'

As the writer saw it, Symmachus's challenge to Ambrose was still awaiting its answer after the passage of more than fifteen and a half centuries. The repressive use of physical force, which had been a Christian Roman Imperial Government's retort to Symmachus, had, of course, been no answer at all.[13]

Toynbee agrees with Radhakrishnan's statement as follows:

In a restless and disordered world...we cannot afford to waver in our determination that the whole of Humanity shall remain a united people, where Muslim and Christian, Buddhist and Hindu shall stand together bound by a common devotion not to something behind but to something ahead, not to racial past or geographical unit, but to a great dream of a world society with a universal religion of which the historical faiths are but branches. We must recognize humbly the partial and defective character of our isolated traditions, and seek their source in the generic tradition from which they all have sprung.... In their wide environment, religions are assisting each other to find their own souls and grow to their full stature.... We are slowly realising that believers with different opinions and convictions are necessary to each other to work out the larger synthesis which alone can give the spiritual basis to a world brought together into intimate oneness by Man's mechanical ingenuity.[14]

III

We have two approaches to Toynbee's view of religion: (1)

Toynbee's study of higher religions, and (2) biographical study of Toynbee's spiritual life. Please see the illustration on the next page. Both are the two sides of the same coin. We have to know both of them in order to reach a holistic understanding of his view of religion. The second had been very limited, however, because Toynbee was reticent about his private matters from his feeling of pietas,[15] until the publication of *An Historian's Conscience: The Correspondence of Arnold J. Toynbee and Columba Cary-Elwes, Monk of Ampleforth*, edited by Christian B. Peper (Beacon Press, 1986) and William H. McNeill's *Arnold J. Toynbee: A Life* (Oxford University Press, 1989). Toynbee himself approved the publication of his private matters about ten or fifteen years after his death in a letter to Mr. Peper dated on 24 December 1970.[16] I think, however, that we should deal with this matter with reverence because this realm is his inner sanctuary.

Drawing from biographical information, we can better understand the shift of emphasis from civilizations to higher religions which comes after volume VII, more precisely after p. 420 of *A Study of History* (1954). For seven years from 1939 to 1946, aged 50 to 57, Toynbee underwent bitter ordeals sometimes at the brink of madness and suicide. This period was his purgatory. Through his sincere self-examination and repentance, his moral character and his understanding of history and religion were deepened. Particularly important for Toynbee was his thirty-seven years' relationship with Father Columba, a Catholic monk. In a letter to Father Columba dated 17 January 1944, Toynbee writes as follows:

> —being imprisoned in one of those self-centered states of anguish in which I often start the day. But after breakfast I did break out of it, partly by praying for other people in

An Illustrative Tree of Arnold J. Toynbee's Spiritual Life History
(1889–1975)

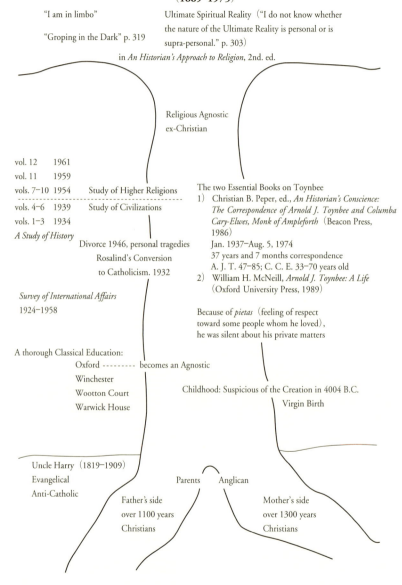

"I am in limbo"

"Groping in the Dark" p. 319

Ultimate Spiritual Reality ("I do not know whether the nature of the Ultimate Reality is personal or is supra-personal." p. 303)

in *An Historian's Approach to Religion*, 2nd. ed.

Religious Agnostic
ex-Christian

vol. 12   1961
vol. 11   1959
vols. 7–10 1954   Study of Higher Religions
vols. 4–6   1939   Study of Civilizations
vols. 1–3   1934
A Study of History

Divorce 1946, personal tragedies
Rosalind's Conversion
to Catholicism. 1932

Survey of International Affairs
1924–1958

A thorough Classical Education:
  Oxford ········· becomes an Agnostic
  Winchester
  Wootton Court
  Warwick House

The two Essential Books on Toynbee
1) Christian B. Peper, ed., *An Historian's Conscience: The Correspondence of Arnold J. Toynbee and Columba Cary-Elwes, Monk of Ampleforth* (Beacon Press, 1986)
Jan. 1937–Aug. 5, 1974
37 years and 7 months correspondence
A. J. T. 47–85; C. C. E. 33–70 years old
2) William H. McNeill, *Arnold J. Toynbee: A Life* (Oxford University Press, 1989)

Because of *pietas* (feeling of respect toward some people whom he loved), he was silent about his private matters

Childhood: Suspicious of the Creation in 4004 B.C.
Virgin Birth

Uncle Harry (1819–1909)
Evangelical
Anti-Catholic

Parents   Anglican

Father's side
over 1100 years
Christians

Mother's side
over 1300 years
Christians

trouble—for one, that poor young farmer at Ganthorpe who has lost his wife—and partly by taking pen in hand and putting a blank sheet of paper under my nose after breakfast. The battle is severe, and I am often forced to the ground, but so far God has helped me, each time, to get up again and go on.[17]

Here we see the personal battle within Toynbee which manifests itself as theoretical transformation that moves his emphasis from civilizations to higher religions.

Religio Historici

In the Preface to the first edition of *An Historian's Approach to Religion,* Toynbee described his subject in the two words *Religio Historici,* following the example of Sir Thomas Browne's

Interpreting President Sentaro Hiroike to Dr. Toynbee, at his London residence on 26, 1972

book *Religio Medici*. *Religio Historici* reveals the whole nature of his view of religion. As his wife Veronica writes in the Preface to the second edition, "His approach to religious problems was an intellectual one. He could not make the final leap into the unverifiable act of faith which could have enabled him to accept, as his own belief and code of practice, Christianity or any of the other higher religions...."[18] His continual pursuit for "the mysteries of the universe and the nature of what he liked to call Ultimate Spiritual Reality"[19] was too strong to stay in the one hold of a particular religion. On July 5, 1994, I had the honor to pay homage to Toynbee's grave in the humble village graveyard near Ganthorpe, Terrington, England, guided by his son Lawrence and his wife Jean. In the sixth of the first row leftside of the entrance stands a simple tomb engraved with the names of Arnold J. Toynbee, CH and Veronica—a humble tomb of a world figure! I knelt before it and deeply prayed. Then a line from Thomas Gray's "Elegy Written in a Country Churchyard" came up to my lips: "The paths of glory lead but to the grave." I rethought, however, that this humble tomb was more appropriate to the modest character of Toynbee. The soul of Toynbee, who overlooked the rises and falls of the thirty-four civilizations of mankind in his lifetime, transcends power and glory on the earth, flying to the Ultimate Spiritual Reality in the twilight universe.

Chapter II

Civilization and Religion

Section 3

The Paths of Spiritual Transmission in Case of Jesus Christ, Gautama Buddha, and Kūkai

I.

The title of my presentation is "The Paths of Spiritual Transmission in case of Jesus Christ, Gautama Buddha, and Kūkai." We have to define, first of all, the meaning of "Spiritual Transmission" briefly before going into discussion. At first, what is spiritual? I mean by spiritual, religious, holy or divine; and secondly more broadly, I mean cultural in general, such as literary, creative and artistic achievements. Why is spiritual transmission necessary? It is because spiritual transmission is essential to elevate a certain level of society to a higher kind of society. Next, where are the fields in which spiritual transmissions are to occur? They occur between God and individual, between individuals, between an individual and society. Thirdly the ways of diffusion should be mentioned. The fourth I will emphasize the significance of spiritual transmission in contemporary civilizations.

II. Transfiguration

Our main theme of this congress is "the Paths of History," and therefore, we should discuss the Spiritual Transmission in the context or framework of comparative study of civilizations. Toynbee writes: "Primitive societies are in a static condition, whereas the civilization or, at any rate, the growing civilizations...are in dynamic movement." (III, 242)[1] A static primitive society was elevated by the spiritual sparks by, using the Toynbee's term, "creative minorities." Henre Bergson writes: "Henceforward, the soul [of the great mystic] has a superabundance of life; it has an immense *élan*; it has an irresistible thrust which hurls it into vast enterprises.... The great mystic has felt the flow into him from its source like a force in action." (III, 234) from Bergson, H.: *Les Deux Sources de la morale et de la Religion* (Paris 1932, Alcan), pp. 246–51.

Toynbee writes as follows: "The transfiguration of a creative personality is a change in his aspect which, *ex hypothesis*, is perceived in him by fellow human beings; and it can only be perceived by men and women who have associated with him after, as well as before, he has enjoyed the personal spiritual experience of which his transfigured countenance is the outward and visible sign." (III, 248, n. 2) One conspicuous example is Jesus' transfiguration: "And he was transfigured before them, and his face shone like the sun, and his garments became white as light." (Matt. 17: 2)

Another remarkable case is Buddha's physical appearance: Throughout his life, his noble aspect inspired many people with majestic nobility. Paul Carus writes: "The beauty of his youth was transfigured by holiness that surrounded his head like a halo."[2]

After his Enlightenment at the age of 35 under the bo tree, he continued to work for moral purification of all kinds of people such as kings, queens to townspeople and even to harlots until his nirvana at the age of 80. His spirit through words and deeds goes into the depth of mind and heart of the people who have contact with him during his lifetime and henceforth for two thousand five hundred years.

III. Editing and Compilation

Both Jesus and Gautama Buddha walked in a small area of Israel and India respectively, and never used, of course, radio, TV and Internet. I wish I could listen to Jesus' Sermon on the Mount and Buddha's Sermon of fire. Jesus' words are kept among his disciples and followers and much later after his death on the cross, his words are compiled in the four gospels.

In India after Buddha's death, compilations were carried out four times: the first was done immediately after his death under Mahākāśyapa with 500 bhiksus, in the suburbs of Rājagrha; Upali, recited laws, Ānanda recited Sūtras. The second was made 100 years later than his death. The third was made 200 years after his death under King Asoka, the fourth compilation meeting was carried out in the second century under King Kaniska.

Before Gutenberg's invention of the printing press, no two copies of a book were the same. When we think of the problem of spiritual transmission in ancient times, we have to keep in mind this kind of technical problem. Fred Gladstone Bratton writes:

"The books of the Bible as first written—the Old Testament books on skins, the New Testament on papyrus—

disappeared not long after their composition. But they were copied, and our only knowledge of their content comes from the study of manuscript copies or copies of copies.... The loss of the original books of the Bible has led to a science called Textual or Lower Criticism."[3]

IV. Missionaries and Churches

Once the Spiritual was established in a few persons, it must have spread through some missionaries such as St. Paul.

Whenever I read St. Paul's missionary work in the Bible since my university days, I could not help being moved by his great sincerity:

> serving the Lord with all humility and with tears and with trials which befell me through the plots of the Jews; (Acts 20: 19)
> "But I do not account my life of any value nor as precious to myself, if only I may accomplish my course and the ministry which I received from the Lord Jesus, to testify the gospel of the grace of God." (Acts 20: 24)

In his missionary journey he met many difficulties:

> "I am talking like a fool—with far greater labors, far more imprisonments, with countless beatings, and often near death. Five times I have received at the hands of the Jews the forty lashes less one.
> Three times I have been beaten with rods: once I was stoned. Three times I have been shipwrecked; a night and a day I have been adrift at sea; on frequent journeys, in danger from rivers, danger from robbers, danger from my

own people, danger from Gentiles, danger in the city, danger in the wilderness, danger at sea, danger from false brethren; in toil and hardship, through many a sleepless night, in hunger and thirst, often without food, in cold and exposure." (2 Corinthians 11: 23–27)

A modern Christian apologist vigorously praises St. Paul's journey:

"Paul did not travel for travel's sake; he traveled to preach—to stir up men, to bring conviction to human hearts, to assault the strongholds of paganism, to do everything in his power, by the grace of God, for the deliverance of men from the bondage of darkness.... Frankly, my fellow believers and fellow preachers, even when we do travel to preach, what happens in the great cities we visit? Nothing! A morning audience of people already Christians, a delicious dinner, a few kind words, a generous check, and we go on our way. What does the city know of our coming? Nothing!.... But this man Paul, when he went into a city, turned it upside down, riots broke out.... Through this man paganism was dealt a death blow. Look at that map—Colosse, Ephesus, Corinth, Thessalonica, Philippi, Lystra, Derbe, everywhere great and flourishing churches, with bishops, before the end of the century!"[4]

V. Translation

St. Paul is no doubt the greatest missionary in the West. In order to keep and spread the initial spiritual sparks to foreign countries, they must be translated into foreign languages. I would like to write about the introduction of Buddhism from

India to China, from Sanskrit to Chinese. The First is Kumārajīva (344–413) and the other is Xuan-Zang (c. 602–664). Kumārajīva was born in Kusha, now Sinkiang province in China. When his mother, a Kuchean princess, became a nun, he followed her into a monastic life at the age of seven. He grew up in centers of Hinayāna Buddhism in his teens. From 401 he was at the Ch'in court in the capital Chang-an (now Sian), where he taught and translated 35 parts 297 volumes of scriptures, including *Saddharmapuṇḍarīka-sūtra*.[5] His Chinese translation of this sūtra is the most famous and influential. On my desk now sit three volumes of his Chinese translation and modern Japanese translation from the original Sanskrit sūtra, I confess I feel his Chinese is more dignified and beautiful, elegant, magnificent, in sound and Chinese letters. It is a miraculous fact that we could manage to read directly his translation from about 1600 years ago.

The other great Chinese translator of Buddhist sūtras in Sanskrit is Xuan-Zang. A Chinese priest, Xuan-Zang traveled to India in 629 to seek Buddhist sūtras and brought them back to China in 645 and he translated 1,335 volumes of sūtras into Chinese with his disciples. His translations were said to be faithful to the Sanskrit original. His travelogue to seek Buddhist sūtras in India was romanticized in *Xi-you-ji* which is very popular even among Japanese children.

Before his Translation work he had to seek authentic scriptures in India. His pilgrimage to India is described in *Da-tang xi-yuji* (646) which is the most accurate description of 138 countries in India and central Asia in the seventh century.

Another spiritual transmission occurred between Hui guo, a Chinese priest and his Japanese student, Kūkai (774–835) in Chang-an, at that time an international capital. Their meetings were short, but Kūkai inherited Esoteric Buddhism and related tools and instruments. He was in a sense, a deep psychologist: he described detailed explorations of ten stages of religious and moral minds:

Ishō-teiyō-shin, an unenlightened man absorbed in satisfying desires; *gudō-jisai-shin*, a foolish child trying to keep precepts; *yōdō-muishin*, the boldness of a child, seeking rebirth in heaven while turning his back on this world; *yuiun-muga-shin*, one who believes that there are only *skandhas* (aggregates) and no ātman (self); *batsugō -inshu-shin*, one who seeks to pull out the seeds to *karman* (destiny); *taen-daijō-shin*, the Mahayanist who contemplates the various causes seeking enlightenment; *kakushin-fushō-shin*, one who meditates on mind and understands the principle of *śūnyatā* (relativity); ichido-muishin, one who walks the single path; *gokumujishō-shin*, one who fathoms the mujishō (having no peculiar nature of its own) doctrine, and *himitsu-shōgon-shin*, one who has attained the secret teaching. (See *Japanese-English Buddhist Dictionary*, Daito-Shuppansha, 1965)

He probed the depth of the mind with the incantation of a sūtra, and his physical appearance changed into a shining body of Mahāvairocana when he was debating other hostile priests. He was well-versed in Sanskrit and Chinese, and his Chinese style was superb. He worked hard for the betterment of people by building bridges, digging wells, making ponds for agriculture, and founding the first private university in Japan. Kūkai's Esoteric Buddhism is sometimes associated with magical powers, incantations, lighting a holy fire for invocation, and it is believed that he has been living in meditation on Mt. Kōya and would be waiting for the coming of Maitreya Boghisattva 5.67 billion years in the future.

Chang-an was an international capitol on Tang Dynasty, where believers of Manichaeism, Nestorianism, Zoroastrianism were living, and where old and new knowledges were available. Communication network, traffic network, bureaucratic systems, and so forth existed and Kūkai was benefitted from that city. Toynbee detailed the relationship between universal states and universal churches, and he succinctly writes: "the principal beneficiaries of universal states are universal churches" (VII, 381). In the previous part of this essay I emphasized the importance of spirit, but I should also here emphasize the serviceability of universal states.

I have been tracing routes of spiritual transmissions intermittently. The main theme of this congress is the paths of history, and I think the essence of the paths of history is a path of spiritual transmission embodying missionaries and the forms of holy scriptures. The road to Damascus is absolutely needed in the time of Civilizational Disintegration.

Chapter III

Civilizations and Morals

Chapter III

Civilizations and Morals

Section 1

Legitimacy, the Line of Succession, and Polity

I

In any society, its leaders and people seek legitimacy. Without legitimacy, a state, group or family cannot have prestige and dignity. Toynbee observes the significance of legitimacy in the case of a universal state as follows:

> ...it is an extraordinary testimony to the attractive power of the institution that it could also be an object of awe and devotion to the internal and external proletariats who had had little part in its construction. On the strength of this fact, both the legitimate holders and the alien usurpers of the sovereign authority in a universal state may, by stressing a genuine or pretended historic right to that authority, retain a considerable status as the sole dispensers of *legitimacy* long after they have lost all real power over their nominal empire.[1][Italics added]

Robert N. Bellah in his book, *The Broken Covenant* also

discussed legitimation [he uses this word instead of legitimacy] in the context of American history, especially in the "Afterword: Religion and the Legitimation of the American Republic."[2] The meaning of this title can be understood from the following statement by the author: "The Pilgrim fathers had a conception of the covenant and of virtue which we badly need today. But almost from the moment they touched American soil they broke that covenant and engaged in unvirtuous actions."[3] *The Broken Covenant* was also "indeed a jeremiad intended to change America."[4]

Ancient Chinese history is related to this because I believe that it can be one of the fundamental measures to judge legitimacy and succession from a historical perspective.

The Three Manners of Succession of the Throne in Ancient China: the Rule of Virtue, the Rule of Right, and the Rule of Might: 帝道 (*Shan*, 禅), 王道 (*Rang*, 譲), and 覇道 (*Fang*, 放 and *Fa*, 伐).

In spite of the 'Announcement of Zhong Hui (仲虺之誥),' King Tang's revolution became both an archetype and an excuse for future revolutions. Chikuro Hiroike summarizes this fact as follows:

> Emperors Yao and Shun did not transfer their thrones to their sons, but abdicated and left them in the hands of virtuous men. When a sovereign turns his throne over to a virtuous man, such abdication of the throne is called *shan*.
>
> On the other hand, Yu passed his throne to his son who was wise enough to hold it. This is no other than the demise of the Crown (*rang*) in the context of the law of succession in terms of modern law.

Tang expelled King Jie from Xia by force and made himself the sovereign (*fang*). Tang was ashamed, however, of his own lack of virtue and made Zhong Hui compose an announcement, as is recorded in the *Shang Shu*.

King Wen of Zhou was powerful enough to control two-thirds of the then world; he dared not revolt against the lawless King Zhou of Yin. His successor King Wu, however, was obliged to attack and destroy King Zhou (*fa*). Because of this, he was opposed by Bo Yi and Shu Qi, contemporary quasi-sages.

Such abdication, as to leave it in the hands of a virtuous man, which is named *shan*, belongs to 'the rule of virtue,' while the other forms of succession mentioned above belong to 'the rule of right.' Confucius, however, considered that "the essential significance of the two are the same." Thus, in China, even expatriation (*fang*) and destruction (*fa*), as far as they are carried out in the context I mentioned earlier, have been regarded in accordance with supreme morality. In contrast, supreme morality in Japan is more strict in this respect: it would admit neither expatriation nor destruction.

Expatriation and destruction, as Tang once feared, as expressed in the 'Announcement of Zhong Hui,' had a gravely evil influence on the manner of transferring sovereign rights in China, until at last they gave birth to the so-called 'rule of might.' The rule of might, completely ignoring morality, solely resorts to law and military force to gain sovereignty or other rights and interests. This rule of might is found in European countries in the past, and is also reflected in a sense in the political situations of today's constitutional states. In China, the age of the rule of might paved the way to the turbulent Age of Warring States. During that Age all people of all classes in China fought against each other driven by selfish desires—lords against vassals, parents against children, forgetting all affection and sense of debt and gratitude, until it seemed as if all humanity was giving way to bestiality. It was in such confusion and corruption when Mencius appeared.... The view that law and power are everything, however, did not only sway China in the Age of Warring States; it is, indeed, as rampant now throughout the constitutional states and republics of the world.[5]

Democracy

A parallel can be drawn with the American presidency. George Washington was regarded as a rebel from the British point of view. The American War of Independence began in 1775 with the firing, at Concord, Massachusetts, of "the shot heard round the World."[6] It was not a mere revolt against George III. Bernard Bailyn says, "Its original aims were quite narrowly political and constitutional: a protest movement against the misuse of power and the violation of constitutional principles by the ministry of George III."[7]

The result was, however, a revolution against England (including George III). If you read "The Declaration of Independence" from the beginning to the end, you will find that its main body consists of 26 items of accusation against George III. Jefferson and his coauthors had to justify the American War of Independence and to establish the legitimacy of American Independence. This situation reminds me of Confucius who from necessity approved Tang of the Yin Dynasty and Wu of the Zhou Dynasty by saying that their revolutions were essentially helpful for the welfare of the people. Yet George Washington was a man of noble character. When he was offered a Crown, he reportedly angrily rejected it. If he had accepted it America might have been a monarchy. Because he rejected the Crown,

America became a republic.

American presidents, ideally, should reflect the continuous rule of virtuous men: from one virtuous President to another. Washington, Jefferson, Lincoln, Wilson, and others were great Presidents. In practice, however, such a scholar as James Bryce addresses the issue, "Why great men are not chosen Presidents"[8] and finds some defects in the Presidency. One of them is "that the presidential election, occurring once in four years, throws the country for several months into a state of turmoil, ..."[9] which "produces a discontinuity of policy."[10]

The presidential election system reminds us of the continuation of prosperity through the symbolic regicide, vividly described by James Frazer in *The Golden Bough*. He writes of the reason for regicide as follows:

> To guard against these catastrophes it is necessary to put the king to death while he is still in the full bloom of his divine manhood, in order that his sacred life, trasmitted in unabated force to his successor, may renew its youth....[11]

The presidential election is, of course, not as violent as described above. Indeed, some critics say that it is conducted by ballots instead of bullets. While democracy can sometimes contain some violent elements, we can say, nevertheless, that a savage regicide has been turned into a more peaceful institution of the presidential election: The American presidency is a firmly established political institution.

Chaotic Society

In some other parts of the world, however, people are struggling to establish legitimate institutions on political soil where the concept of legitimacy is blurred, ambiguous, or not easily found. Reinhard Bendix writes as follows:

> In the twentieth century, the people's ultimate sovereignty in the new states suffers from weak political institutions.... The emotional foundation of a political community is missing in the new states, whose people typically share collective memories only of colonial domination and now of the struggle against it.[12]

Monarchy

Japanese monarchy, in contrast, has been enjoying an unbroken line of succession over two millennia. Bendix writes, "Japan is a unique case, since for a millennium its governmental and ceremonial authority had been divided."[13] Robert E. Ball, former Chief Chancery Master, writes that Japan has had a double kingship, i.e., Emperor and Shogun or Emperor and Prime Minister.[14] This system is well-balanced and stable. Robert Bellah writes, "Most Christian political theorists down through the ages have considered monarchy the best form of gorvernment (Christan religious symbolism would seem to be much more monarchical than republican)."[15]

II

I have discussed the three types of succession and three polities, or political systems: democracy, chaotic society, and monarchy. People forget or lose sight of the concepts of legitimacy, the line of succession, and polity. I think whether or not we keep these concepts and measures in mind is related to our behavior. President Clinton, in his "State of the Union Address," on January 23, 1996, urged Americans to build stronger families and thus a stronger America, and warned against the bad influence of movies, CDs, televison shows, and the teen pregnancy rate. His warning is quite applicable to many countries, including Japan. I would like to introduce Dr. Chikuro Hiroike's idea of ortholinon as an antidote to a too-democratic, or a too-egocentric society.

Hiroike presents the concept of *ortholinon*. Etymologically, ortholinon is derived from the Greek word *orthos*, meaning "straight," and *linon*, meaning "thread." Hiroike coined this word in order to denote the lines of benefactors, common to mankind, who have contributed to the realization of human existence, development, security, peace and happiness. The fundamental spirit of the ortholinon is derived from God, who created and nourishes all things. Ortholinon may be divided into three main kinds.

Family Ortholinons: our parents and ancestors, the benefactors of family life, and the source of our life and those who have raised us.

National Ortholinons: the line of benefactors for national life. The independence and security of a state are indispensable elements, not only for the foundation of national life, but also for the establishment of international peace. Any given nation has its national ortholinon, a being who performs the central role in maintaining unity. In Japan, the national ortholinon is the Emperor, who is the symbol of national unity; but in general the national ortholinon is represented by the head of state, such as the king or the president of the county in question, according to the differences of the history of the respective nations.

Spiritual Ortholinons: the benefactors in spiritual life, i.e., the lines of the men of supreme morality, such as the sages, as well as those who bring about enlightenment and salvation according to the teachings of the sages. The ideas and doctrines of the sages have been inherited and developed in the form of philosophies and religions. The teachings of Socrates in Greece and those of Confucius in China developed as philosophies, and the teachings of Buddha in India and those of Christ in Judea developed in the form of religions. The two streams of those philosophies and religions have elucidated the ultimate goal of mankind and have become the sources of remarkable human cultures. Transcending differences of nationality, philosophy, and religion, we respect those benefactors as spiritual ortholinons.

Quasi-Ortholinons: In addition to the three types of ortholinon already mentioned, there are certain kinds of benefactors in our social life. They are called quasi-ortholinons.[16]

III

Yet Benjamin R. Barber claims that "for true democracy to flourish, there must be citizens. Citizens are women and men educated for excellence." True democracy cannot stand without "universal education in excellence, creating an aristocracy of everyone." Barber is aware that "an aristocracy of everyone" sounds to be "a provocative oxymoron," but he believes that "everyone is regarded as possessing a potential for the best."[17] Raymond Croly quotes in his *The Promise of American Life* (New York: Macmillan, 1909), p. 454, the American philosopher George Santayana saying: "If a noble and civilized democracy is to subsist, the common citizen must be something of a saint and something of a hero. We see, therefore, how justly flattering and profound, and at the same time how ominous, was Montesquieu's saying that the principle of democracy is virtue."[18]

We are living in a noisy world which respects equality, freedom, self-reliance, individualism, demand for one's own rights, etc. to an extreme degree, and forgets the importance of loyalty, considerations to others, the precedence of duty over personal rights, self-renunciation, etc. Hiroike's ideas may contribute something moral and noble to such a World.

Rousseau says, "Return to nature." But I say, "Return to the teachings of sages" together with the knowledge of modern science and technology.

Chapter III

Civilizations and Morals

Section 2

Global Ethics in Practice

When we look back to the past centuries, even millennia, from the present moment of A.D. 2000 we can easily now find the great advancements in science and technology and their correspondent increases in wealth, welfare, and convenience. Nevertheless, there are dark sides: the increase in the numbers of conflicts on a larger scale,[1] the deterioration of the environment by nuclear accidents and fallout and industrial waste, etc. We are in a Janus year and a civilizational turning point. We are in need of global ethics in order to cooperate for a better world. In this sense several clauses of the U.N. Universal Declaration of Human Rights are relevant to be quoted here:

"Everyone has the right to life, liberty and the security of person...human beings shall enjoy freedom of speech and belief.... All are equal before the law and are entitled without any discrimination to equal protection.... Everone has the right to a standard of living adequate for the health and well-being of himself and of his family, including food, clothing, housing and medical care necessary social services.... Everyone has the right to education."

In the same line of reasoning, Professor Harrison believes that "the vast majority of the planet's people would agree with the following assertions:

> Life is better than death.
> Health is better than sickness.
> Liberty is better than slavery.
> Prosperity is better than poverty.
> Education is better than ignorance.
> Justice is better than injustice."[2]

The above seem to be, and should be, rules of global ethics. It is, however, difficult for one to apply these rules practically in a particular time and place. The problem is not so simple as it appears.

Before global ethics there must be various forms of local ethics, tribal ethics, national ethics, etc., all of which are also needed. The reason why there are various forms of ethics which apply to a various cultural domains lies in the fact that "ethics" originally comes from manners and customs. Each part of the world has its own particular mores, manners, and customs, which means, therefore, each place has its own particular ethics. The problem is how to cooperate and develop both types of ethics at practical level.

When we think of global ethics directly, we naturally think of an ethics as the greatest common divisor, such as "Do not kill," and "Do not steal." But when we think over the following questions which Dr. Edward Tivnan raises, it is not so easy:

Is abortion murder? What about your father suffering the interminable pain of cancer—should you help him die? Is capital punishment more than mere vengeance? Should an African-American be given special consideration for employment or educational opportunities, even of a white candidate is better qualified?[3]

Tivnan raises five difficult moral issues: abortion, suicide, euthanasia, and racism. The first four issues are related to "killing" and the last is to discrimination. He examines the pros and the cons of each issue, and finally reaches a relative point of view. For example, Tivnan introduces a disagreement about the morality of abortion by the best informed and most thoughtful couple who are happily married: Sidney Callahan, a professor of psychology at Mercy College in New York, who opposes abortion, and her husband, Daniel Callahan, a pioneer in medical ethics and the founding director of the Hastings Institute, who is pro-choice.[4] There have been many controversies whether the fetus is a person or not, or in what stage the fetus becomes a person. After describing the pros and the cons concerning abortion, and experiencing agonizing conversations, Tivnan concludes that, the right-to-life camp has hypocrites among its number, and some are my friends; (2) women, even upper-middle-class, well-educated women with loving, sympathetic husbands, are not always free in sexual and procreative matters; and (3) abortion will never be only a theoretical debate. It is a blood and guts issue, particularly for women.... To claim to have resolved the issue once and for all is foolish.[5] He further laments: "Moral conflict is inevitable in the United States, where people's fundamental religious, ideological, and ethical positions are bound to clash with the opinions of others from different traditions."[6] Tivnan's final conclusion is that we are required to stretch "the moral imagination."

In *The Good Society*, Robert Bellah discusses this problem from a broader perspective, i.e., from the comparative study of the laws of abortion in America and twenty Western democracies as follows:

> Comparing the laws about abortion in twenty Western democracies, [Mary Ann] Glendon points out that the United States is anomalous in both its policies and the way it frames the issue. Only in the United States are the laws framed with abortion seen as a matter of rights—the abstract rights of the fetus versus the right of a woman to control her own body. This formulation, Glendon argues, has led to an all-or-nothing approach; either the fetus is a person, whose right to life is absolute (except when the life of the mother is directly threatened), or the fetus is not a person in which case the woman's right to an abortion is absolute and not subject to social intervention. In many European societies, Glendon notes, the laws acknowledge the fetus as a life that deserves social protection, but this does not endow the fetus with an absolute 'right' to be born. Instead, the government's general obligation to protect first requires positive social policies that allow women to afford to bear and rear children; second, courts and other government agencies can balance the life of the unborn child against the needs of the mother and other social goods (the dangers of unwanted children, battered children, or illegal abortions). In such societies abortions are legal, but the decision to abort is not the woman's absolute right.[7)]

The above sounds to be maturer and well-balanced, but this still remains on the level of a policy, not of a personal inner satisfaction.

We have discussed only the abortion issue, and find that it is very difficult or impossible to reconcile the two opposing camps. And so it is impossible to find a global ethics concerning abortion, that is, if we remain in an analytical position, paying attention only to the limited realm of abortion.

Let us think about human nature.

A mother's painful experience concerning her aborted child could hardly be alleviated by mere ethical theories. An elderly director of obstetrics in an abortion clinic in Tokyo was reported to have seen a fantastic vision of thousands of aborted babies swarming around him in his dying hour. "Forgive and help me" were his last words.[8] This is almost Hawthornesque. In one of his early tales, "Alice Doane's Appeal" (1835), Nathaniel Hawthorne writes as follows:

> Each family tomb had given up its inhabitants, who, one by one, through distant years, had been borne to its dark chamber, but now came forth and stood in a pale group together. There was the gray ancestor, the aged mother, and all their descendants, some withered and full of years, like themselves, and others in their prime; there, too were the children who went prattling to the tomb, and there the maiden who yielded early beauty to death's embrace, before passion had polluted it.[9]

In Hawthorne's "Young Goodman Brown" (1835), the devil says,

> How fair damsels—blush not, sweet ones!—have dug little graves in the garden, and bidden me, the sole guest to an

infant's funeral. By the sympathy of your human hearts for sin, ye shall scent out all the places—whether in church, bed-chamber, street, field, or forest—where crime has been committed, and shall exult to behold the whole earth one stain of guilt, one mighty blood-spot.[10]

Hawthorne's imagination stretches from this world to the past and the other world. Dante also visioned people in Hell. If our imagination could stretch our present life to our before-and-after lives, we could live more thoughtfully. Nathaniel Hawthorne is a nineteenth century American writer who wrote about the seventeenth century Puritans in New England, and I am a Japanese of the 20th–21st centuries; but I can share this kind of imagination with Hawthorne across the gulf of time and culture, because he dug the depth of common human heart and the reality of life. Hawthorne probes into universal human sin.

There may be some differences of external attitudes towards abortion in each culture; however, at least we share a common possibility of guilty consciousness. In some Buddhist temples in Japan, for example, they have a mass for aborted or miscarried babies. When I happened to visit a certain Buddhist temple, I found in a corner of the precinct many nursing bottles, hundreds of dolls, pretty children's clothes, etc., offered in front of the guardian deity for the spirits of aborted children.

Let us, then, seek another perspective to find a global ethics. If we are entangled in these technicalities, we cannot reach a satisfactory answer. Rather we have to trace the depth and origin of the problem in human nature itself. Many religions and philosophies have pointed to the common conclusion that there are selfishness, sin, doxa, and stain in human nature. All these are the origin of sufferings. Therefore, we have to cleanse our soul and make a conversion from the sinful state of mind through the teachings of the sages. Without recreating our moral character, any opinion will not lead us to happiness.

Secondly, in order to lead our civilizations to a higher species of civilization (Toynbee), we must put our foundation on God, or the ultimate spiritual reality, whatever name that may be. Samuel P. Huntington writes as follows:

> At least at a basic "thin" morality level, some commonalities exist between Asia and the West. In addition, as many have pointed out, whatever the degree to which they divided humankind, the world's major religions—Western Christianity, Orthodoxy, Hinduism, Buddhism, Islam, Confucianism, Taoism, Judaism—also share key values in common. If humans are ever to develop a universal civilization, it will emerge gradually through the exploration and expansion of these commonalities.[11]

Lao-tsu, a legendary Chinese philosopher of the sixth century B.C., wrote *Lao-tsu's (Tao Te Ching) Morality Sutra*, which Joseph Needham considers to be "without exception the most profound and beautiful work in the Chinese language."[12]

The first paragraph starts as follows:

The Tao that can be told is not the eternal Tao.
The name that can be named is not the eternal name.
The nameless is the beginning of heaven and earth.
The named is the mother of ten thousand things.[13]

What people regard as the Way to follow is not an unchangeable way. What poeple regard as names which they think right is expedient. In the beginning of Heaven and Earth, there was no name. The names of Heaven and Earth were born only after Heaven and Earth, which are the mothers of every thing, became existent.[14] When we read Lao-tsu, we are relieved from day-to-day rules of conduct, and immersed into nameless and spiritual being. Lao-tsu expounds the importance of transcending all the relative and discriminative views, and teaches us about identifying ourselves with the Absolute.

Recently I read Shuntaro Ito's *Nature*[15] in which he examines the concepts of Greek physis, Arabic tabia, Latin nature, European nature, Chinese 自然 (*ziran*), and suggests that our concept of nature is closely related to the maintenance of the environment of the earth. The origin of physis is birth, growth, and becoming. In ancient Greece, physis was akin to human beings. Arabic tabia has a meaning of creation. In Islam, nature (tabia) is always considered in connection with the divine creation. In the view of nature in medieval Christianity, oneness of God, man, and nature are broken down. The Creator and creature are separated. Bacon expresses of the idea of nature which could be controlled and utilized by human beings. If we take the view of nature by Descartes, i.e. the mechanical and cold view of nature, we are led to damage nature. We are obliged to reconsider Descartes's mechanical view of nature and Bacon's view of control of nature in connection of environmental problems today. Chinese *ziran* is as it is, autonomy, voluntary nature. In Japan, nature means radical ties between nature and human beings. Japanese concept of radical ties between nature and human beings should be considered in connection with European "deep ecology," Professor Ito concludes. This is my very rough summary of Ito's profound book. This is the task of the comparative study of civilizations, and which is very helpful in creating a global ethics in many fields.

Lastly as Karl Jaspers says, we had an Axial Period in 800–300 B.C.; the second Axial Period is to be anticipated. We are required to have ancient moral and religious wisdom and at the same time knowledge of advanced science and technology. The task of the comparative study of civilizations is to synthesize these two, and should be instrumental in bringing a new integrated and enlightened Civilization.

Chapter III

Civilizations and Morals

Section 3

Toward Common Wisdom

Many people who read Samuel Huntington's *The Clash of Civilizations and the Remaking of World Order* criticize the "Clash," but do not pay enough attention to the latter half, "Remaking of the World Order." Of course we oppose the clash of civilizations and its subsequent destruction of civilizations. And the Author does not encourage the clash of civilizations, but he hopes for the Remaking of World Order.

He writes on page 320 as follows:

> At least at a basic "thin" morality level, some commonalities exist between Asia and the West. In addition, as many have pointed out, whatever the degree to which they divided humankind, the world's major religions—Western Christianity, Orthodoxy, Hinduism, Buddhism, Islam, Confucianism, Taoism, Judaism—also share key values in common. If humans are ever to develop a universal

civilization, it will emerge gradually through the exploration and expansion of these commonalities. Thus, in addition to the abstention rule and the joint mediation rule, the third for peace in a multicivilizational world is the *commonalities rule:* peoples in all civilizations should search for and attempt to expand the values, institutions, and practices they have in common with peoples for other civilizations.

This effort would contribute not only to limiting the clash of civilizations but also to strengthening Civilization in the singular (hereafter capitalized for clarity). The singular Civilization presumably refers to a complex mix of higher levels of morality, religion, learning, art, philosophy, technology, material well-being, and probably other things.

To Huntington's proposal, I would like to respond in the form of 'Higher Religions' and 'Supreme Morality.'

'Higher Religions,' is a phrase coined by Arnold J. Toynbee, who studied civilizations in the history of humankind, and in his later years he shifted his focus from civilizations to higher religions, and envisaged "a higher species of society" beyond civilizational societies. 'Supreme Morality,' is a term created by Chikuro Hiroike, who studied the highest moral principles commonly existing in the teachings and practices of the five world sages and verified their rationality by means of the principles of modern science covering the three fields of the natural and social sciences and the humanities. Hiroike systematized the results into a new moral science, "moralogy." He intended moralogy to be "special science that constitutes "a foundation for the realization of lasting peace in the world." (SM I, 49)[1] He also envisaged "a higher state of civilization." (SM III, 187)

I. Higher Religions

The phrase 'higher religions' refers to religions in which it is possible for human beings to directly and characteristically enter into a relationship with the Ultimate Spiritual Reality within, behind, and beyond the Universe.   Concrete societal examples are, for example, the 'Church' of Christianity, and the 'Sangha' of Buddhism.   Toynbee, in his *magnum opus, A Study of History*,[2] lists more than 29 of the higher religions which have appeared in the history of humankind, and in his *An Historian's Approach to Religion*,[3] he identifies three stages of religions.

The first is the worship of nature.

The second he calls man-worship, and he further subcategorizes this into three parts:

1. the idolization of parochial communities,
2. the idolization of an ecumenical community, and
3. the idolization of a self-sufficient philosopher.

The final stage is the epiphany of the higher religions. Each higher religion is made up of two kinds of ingredients: essential counsels and truths and non-essential practices and propositions.   People seeking understanding of the absolute truths must temporarily 'tune into' the environment.   At such times additional elements are acquired by chance.   For example, local holy places, rituals, taboos, myths, the poetic and scientific usage of language, conflicts between different social conventions: celibacy versus marriage, monogamy versus polygamy, stringency in the Christian versus laxity in the Muslim regulation of divorce, caste versus the brotherhood of all believers.[4]   Having discarded these, however, the essence of what remains of each of these religions has, as common features, the renunciation of selfcenteredness, and the seeking for the

Ultimate Spiritual Reality.

Toynbee recognizes the diversity of higher religions. The reason why we believe in a particular religion is mostly historical accident: we are destined to be born and brought up in a particular time and place. God or the Ultimate Spiritual Reality is infinite and transcends all our human understanding. In order to understand It, It must be reflected through a particular time and place, a particular language and culture, a particular eye and the vision of a particular human being. When a man catches God or Ultimate Spiritual Reality, it is only a part of it, not all of it. Toynbee maintains, therefore, claiming to possess a monopoly of the Divine Light is *hubris*. Toynbee mentions the name of Quintus Aurelius Symmachus (c. 345–c. 405), whenever he needs to explain his personal religious view and his attitude toward higher religions in general. Symmachus was a Roman government official and orator who argued for the retention of the old Roman religion in official state functions, but was successfully opposed by St. Ambrose.... [But] "Symmachus's challenge to Ambrose was still awaiting its answer after the passage of more than fifteen and a half centuries. The repressive use of physical force, which had been a Christian Roman Imperial Government's retort to Symmachus, had, of course, been no answer at all."[5]

Toynbee writes as follows:

> I am not entitled to call myself a Christian; I must call myself a Symmachan.

Symmachus's confession of faith—"The heart of so great a mystery can never be reached by following one road only"—is an article in my creed which neither my head nor my heart will allow me to abandon.'[6] Toynbee's inner battle was first revealed in *An Historian's Conscience: The Correspondence of Arnold J. Toynbee and Columba Cary-Elwes, Monk of Ampleforth*,[7] and then, William H. McNeill's *Arnold J. Toynbee: A Life*.[8] After reading the above two books, we can understand why Toynbee shifted his focus from civilization to religion between volume 6 and volume 7 of *A Study of History*. Volume 7 *Universal Churches* is his study of higher religions which extends 775 pages long. In connection with our theme, "In Pursuit of Common Morality in a Global Age," volume 7, III. (a) the sections of "The Higher Religion's Consensus and Dissension," "The Causes of the Dissension and the Prospects of Transcending it," and "The Value of Diversity,"[9] are important. For example, he writes, "...if the followers of the living higher religions were to recognize reciprocally the common origin of all these gifts of God, they might win a life-giving liberation..." (442–443)[10] and "The spiritual insight that they might gain through further suffering might lead them, as we have suggested, to a mutual recognition of their own essential unity in diversity" (p. 448).[11] As a conclusion I may summarize the section of Toynbee as follows:

1. The diversity of higher religions—tolerance to other religions
2. Getting to know each other
3. "four variations on a single theme" (of four higher religions)[12]
4. Because he was not an ethicist, he did not formulate a system of morality. But he found the common ground—the renunciation of self and belief in the Ultimate Spiritual Reality.
5. For the salvation of humankind, he envisaged the distinct species of society beyond civilization.

II. Supreme Morality

Chikuro Hiroike, on the other hand, in his discourse on the sages that forms part of his *Towards Supreme Morality* (the original title is *A Treatise on Moral Science* (chapter 12, section 2)), says that 'There are five great systems of supreme morality in the world.' In section 3, he summarizes the requirements of the sage and the quasi-sage. They are studies of Socrates, Jesus Christ, Buddha, Confucius, and Amaterasu Ōmikami. Some of the followers of the five sages may be offended by the calling their founder a sage, but please allow us to use the term "sage" in the meaning of "those who have practiced supreme morality." The order of the description of the five sages is "from west to east without discrimination." (T II, 147)

The Principles Which Hiroike Draws from his Study of the Five Sages

Hiroike expounds essentials in each sage's teachings and practices, which he thinks contribute to the principles of supreme morality. I pick up here principles, or items of which, Hiroike thought, are related to supreme morality, found in each sage's teachings.

Socrates (469–399 B.C.)
1. The problem of truth. "He saw clearly that the prevailing ethical and political fallacies sprang from a total misconception of the meaning of truth and that the problem of knowledge was the key to the entire situation." (T II, 151)
2. Socrates believed in τὸ δαιμόνιον (daimonion), something like god. (T II, 160)

3. Socrates defended the National Ortholinon* at the risk of his life. T II, 161). His moving conversation with Crito on respecting law and justice. (T II, 161–164)

   * Ortholinon is an important moralogical term, and it is convenient for us to explain this term here. "Ortholinon coined from the Greek words *orthos* (straight) and *linon* (thread) by Hiroike, literally means "line of succession." It denotes the lines of benefactors common to mankind who have contributed to the realization of human existence, development, and happiness. The fundamental spirit of the ortholinon is considered to be derived from God. Ortholinon may be divided into three kinds: family ortholinons meaning the benefactors of family life, i.e. parents and ancestors; national ortholinons meaning the line of benefactors for national life including the heads of state, and the spiritual ortholinons meaning the benefactors in spiritual life including the sages and their faithful followers devoting themselves to the enlightenment and salvation of people" (T II, 161). The principle of ortholinon is discussed in T III, 111–185.

4. Selflessness
5. Plato and Aristotle

Jesus Christ
1. His life—the Meaning of Christ, Virgin Birth, Salvation, the Sermon on the Mount, the God of Christ's Belief, God in the Old Testament, Anthropomorphism, Jehovah, the development of the idea of God, Revelation, the Divine Trinity, Repentance, Conversion, Atonement, and Regeneration, Righteousness and Love
2. Christ's Respect for His Ortholinon (T II, 191)
3. The Problem of the Messiah (T II, 194)
4. The Causes of the Crucifixion, with Descriptions of the Event (T II, 196–210)
5. Rise of Christian Theology—Christianity and Classical Culture, Scholastic Philosophy, Early Theology, Gnostics, Apologists, logos-doctrine, Paul

Śākyamuni

1. The relation between Śākyamuni and Buddha, Tathagata, Tathagata Mahavairocana, Tathagata Amitabha, and Maitreya
2. Śākyamuni's Birth, Renunciation of the World, Enlightenment, and Nirvana, Śākyamuni's Attainment of Buddhahood (T II, 236–241)
3. The Twelve-linked Chain of Causation, the Four Noble Truths, the Noble Eightfold Path, and the Middle Path (T II, 242–251)
4. The Meaning of Nirvana and Vimukti (Deliverance) (T II, 251–253)
5. The Theory of Trikaya (T II, 253–256)
6. Schisms in Buddhism after Buddha' Death: Theravada, Mahasamghika, Hinayana (Little Vehicle), Mahayana (Great Vehicle)—Provisional Mahayana and Real Mahayana—Teachings on Self-Exertion and Selfless Reliance
7. Śākyamuni Respected His Ortholinons
   Hiroike puts a comment on this as follows: Śākyamuni's conception of ortholinon is idealistic as is Christ's, so in *Shibunritsu (Si Fen Lu or The Vinaya [Rules of Discipline] in Four Divisions)* Śākyamuni states manifestly: "I also have no master." It is different from the concrete conception of ortholinon held by Amaterasu Ōmikami in Japan and Confucius in China. If we study deeply the fundamental principles that underlie these conceptions, however, we may understand that all these are identical in spirit.
   The author's note: —The Buddhist concept of respect for ortholinons made remarkable development late with the teaching of Mahayana, culminating in the Faith of

the Pure Land. Ortholinons in morality and religion are different from teachers of arts and sciences; teachers are of much less importance than ortholinons. (T II, 267)
8. Śākyamuni's Ultimate Ideal—The Pre-eminence of the Mahayana (T II, 273)

Confucius
1. Ortholinons of Supreme Morality in China before Confucius.
   Ortholinons come first characteristically in the section of Confucius, Yao of Tang, Shun of Yu, Yu of Xia, Tang of Shang...
2. Di Dao (the Way of Emperor), Wang Dao (the Way of King) and Ba Dao (the Way of Generalissimo): the Meaning of Shan, Rang, Fang and Fa, or the Meanings of Abdication of the Throne and subjugation of the Throne (T II, 321–331). These four ways of succession in China and the history of Japanese Imperial household have influenced Hiroike's way of thinking.[13]
3. Chapter 12, VII. ii "The descendants of the Ancient Sages" reads "According to the explanations of Confucius, Mencius and Si Ma Qian, the descendants of the performers of supreme morality in China, as far as they were not placed in certain exceptional situations, were to thrive long-lastingly and to develop the fortunes of their families, repeatedly producing among themselves sages or semisages. These explanations agree with the results of recent studies in theories of evolution, genetics, and sociology." (T I, 331) This way of explanation is, however, against some American thought.[14]

4. The Advent of Confucius
5. VII. Iv "How Confucius Respected Ortholinons and How He Perfected Supreme Morality in China." (T II, 344)
6. Confucius's belief in God (T II, 347)

   Hiroike writes, "Confucius believed deeply in God, renounced selfishness completely, ...Those who inherited his learning, however, came by and by to lose his true spirit, until Yang Zi, for instance, came to hold that God is nothing but the human mind. Since then, the spirit of Confucianism has almost died and at last has lost its true moral control over man's minds (T II, 347–348). How to interpret God, Heaven, or the Heavenly Way in China is very important. Hiroike firmly maintains as follows: "The fundamental rule observed by the ancient Chinese sages in their belief and worship of God was that that principle of human development had emerged wholly from that natural law of the universe which they called *Tian Dao*, the Heavenly Way, *Tian Li*, the Heavenly Reason or *Shen Dao*, the Divine Way." (T II, 350)

Hiroike's methodology in chapters 12 and 13 is neither so-called hermeneutics nor exegesis, rather to extract principles and verify them by branches of science. One concrete example is found in the explanation of Shintō's Grand Purification as follows:

> "It is basic to all the main religions of the world that the diseases, disasters and other misfortunes of mankind are the result of defects in mental activity and conduct, that is, sins towards God or crimes against society.... This belief is wholly reasonable when inferred from those scientific

principles introduced in Chapters Three and Four." (T II, 435)

Chapter Three reads "The Given Causes of Man's Division into Classes," (T I, 109–174) and Chapter Four reads "Acquired Causes in the Making of Human Classes." (T I, 175–254) Though Hiroike did not specify which section of each chapter to be referred, it is obvious that the section of mental heredity and so on in Chapter Three and the whole part of Chapter four, and I might add Chapter Five, "The Fundamental Principle concerning the Spiritual and Material Life of Mankind" are implied.

Chapter Five, "The Fundamental Principle concerning the Spiritual and Material Life of Mankind," section III is a conclusion of chapters 12 and 13, that is, it reads "The Doctrine Concerning the Unity of Knowledge and Morality as Found in Socratism, Christianity, Buddhism, Confucianism and Ancient Japanese Thought." (T I, 259–263)

Hiroike does not take literally, nor swallow the discourse and deeds of the sages;[15] for example, though he introduced the renunciation of the world by some sages, he writes in Chapter 14, XI. Ix as follows:

> "There is a theory that those who are going to engage in salvation or to receive it should give up their learning, intellect, wealth, power or high position in society like Śākyamuni, Christ or many founders of religious sects. This theory shows a human weak point, and, in reality, it has been proved true.... Judging from the history of the development of civilization, however, it seems to me no longer impossible today to make people practise supreme morality without so drastically depriving them of their own

individual or social influence." (T III, 307)

Hiroike's intention to establish moralogy as a new moral science is to establish a moral system which transcends the differences of cultures and religions or mores and to offer a universal, or, in a sense, as the theme of this conference shows, the common morality on a scientific basis. As the principle of electricity is applicable in the four corners of the world, the principle of moralogy is applicable in any and all parts of the world.

He made an examination of the history of moral science in the West in Chapter I, "Previous plans to Western Scholars Who Intended to Study Scientifically the Effects of Moral Practice." (T I, 64–66) Among some twenty scholars mentioned there, he showed great sympathy to Leslie Stephen (1832–1904) toward his *The Science of Ethics* (1882), Chapter I, section ii, the 'Difficulty of Moral Science.' This great English Utilitarian scholar points out as follows: "the imperfection of science generally" the hopeless complexity of the problem of individual conduct, "the absence of scientific psychology and in section iii, that the statistical method is insufficient and that the method of political economy is also insufficient." (T I, 64)

We interpret chapters 12 and 13 in the paradigm of moralogy: he is not a Greek philosopher, nor a Christian theologian, nor Buddhist scholar, nor Confucian scholar, nor a Shintō priest, though he was well-versed in each sage.

Let us explore the meaning of supreme morality. The first explanation of supreme morality is as follows:

Supreme morality contains the essence, or the essential principles of thought and morality of the above five moral systems. This is often mistakenly understood as supreme morality is the common ground of the five sages. This interpretation is partially true, but not completely true, because the structure of *Towards Supreme Morality* is organically connected from the first page to the end. Hiroike quotes a passage from *Xun Zi*, Book of Ai Gong as follows:

Confucius says: "...My lord, when you go out of the four gates of the Court and have a view of surrounding suburbs, you will surely find here and there a series of remains of ruined provinces. If you come to think of fear about vicissitudes, why can't you easily imagine how fearful decline is?" (T III, 457–458) When we read this book, we can share the similar poetical feeling with Confucius and Hiroike.

III.

In the connection of our theme, several clauses of the UN Universal Declaration of Human Rights are relevant to be quoted here: "Everyone has the right of life, liberty and the security of person...human beings shall enjoy freedom of speech and belief.... All are equal before the law and are entitled without any discrimination to equal protection.... Everyone has the right to a standard of living adequate for the health and well-being of himself and of his family, including food, clothing housing and medical care necessary social services...everyone has the right to education."

In the same line of reasoning, Professor Harrison believes that "the vast majority of the planet's population would agree with the following assertions:

Life is better than death.
Health is better than sickness.
Liberty is better than slavery.
Prosperity is better than poverty.

Education is better than ignorance.
Justice is better than injustice."[16]

The above seem to be, and should be, rules of global ethics.

Another document to be referred here is "Introduction" and "The Principles of a Global Ethic" made by an Editorial Committee of the Council of the Parliament of the World's Religions in Chicago on the basis of the Declaration composed in Tubingen (here headed 'Principles'), read out publicly at the solemn concluding plenary on 4 September 1993 in Grant Park, Chicago. This is ascribed to by: Bahai, Brahma Kumaris, Buddhism, Christianity, Native Religions, Hinduism, Jainism, Judaism, Islam, Neo-pagans, Sikhs, Taoists, Theosophists, Zoroastrians, Interreligious organizations, etc. I appreciate their effort greatly. This is a kind of ethical constitution of the world; however, there is a problem. Where is enforcement and attractiveness? These kinds of rules are something like distilled water. Harmlessly neutral but no taste.

Is supreme morality a common morality? Logically speaking, "supreme" is superlative, and "common" is ordinary, and so supreme is not common. Therefore supreme morality is not a common morality. But please wait a moment. As I discussed in section II, supreme morality should be considered in the paradigm of moral science. It is not a mere essence of the teachings of the five sages, but the verified principles by sciences. The principles of electricity can be applicable in any corner of the world, so can the principle of moralogy. Supreme morality should be a common morality in the future. In the practice of morality, we need devotion. Anyone who reads chapter 20 of the Acts in the *New Testament* will be moved by St. Paul's devotion. Mere human ethics have no power to elevate us to sainthood. Toynbee writes, "Such sainthood is indispensable for the maintenance of societies—even those of the pettiest and simplest and lowest kind—because even the minimum of unselfishness and determination and courage and vision that is required for making social life possible on Earth far exceeds the range of the natural altruism of a social animal."[17] Hiroike quoted a passage from *Saddharmapuṇḍarīka-sūtra*, "They [Bodhisattvas] have already realized self-interest." (SM II, 278)   Toynbee also says in the same line, "The only heart in which self-interest is truly 'enlightened', and therefore practically effective as a motive for action, is the heart of the saint who identifies his self-interest with the service of God and who therefore sees the field of action from God's angle of vision."[18]

Whenever we looks for points of comparison with Toynbee's '*religio historici*' and Hiroike's combining energy of scientific study of morality and salvational work, we are amazed by their devotion in each field.   There are also many points of spiritual affinity between the two great sage-scholars of both the East and West.

Chapter IV

Two Civilizations and One City

Chapter IV

Two Civilizations and One City

Section 1

My Journey in Search of the Essence of Japanese Civilization

For me it is both an honor to give an opening presentation at this session on "Mainstream Civilizations" chaired by Professor Matthew Melko, and a duty, as a Japanese civilizationist, to focus on the status of Japanese civilization.

Japan is an island country, located east of the Eurasian Continent, and so sometimes compared with England, which is located west of the Eurasian Continent. But the Straits of Dover are narrower than those separating Korea and Japan, which gives Japan a more independent position, though still one where it is has a relationship with Eurasia.

In recent years new archeological discoveries about the *Jomon* and *Yayoi* periods have meant that historians are very busy rewriting ancient Japanese history. The problem remains, though, that wood, the architectural material that was used, rots easily and is also flammable; therefore, no fair comparison is possible with ancient remains elsewhere, such as those of the cities of Mesopotamia, the pyramids of Egypt, the Greek Parthenon and the Roman temples and basilicas. But in any case, in the compass of a short presentation I do not have the time to engage in a comparison of the status of Japanese civilization with other civilizations. So I will limit myself to considering one of its marked moral characteristics, namely its peculiar sense of purity, which is not a matter of mere ablutions, but something which leads to an ever-replacing of the old by the new; an example of this is the complete rebuilding of the Ise Shrines every twenty years, a tradition that dates back thirteen centuries.

The Grand Shrine of Ise (伊勢神宮, *Ise Jingū*), a Shintō shrine dedicated to the goddess Amaterasu Ōmikami, is located in the city of Ise in Mie prefecture, Japan. Officially, it is known simply as *Jingū* (神宮), and its Inner Shrine (*Naiku*), founded about 2000 years ago, as *Kotaijingu*. The main deity enshrined within it is Amaterasu Ōmikami, the ancestress of the Imperial Family and the tutelary *kami* of the Japanese people.

Arnold Toynbee paid a visit to this shrine and left the following short but profound message:

> "Here, in this holy place,
> I feel the underlying unity
> of all religions."
> Arnold Toynbee
> 24 November, 1967
>
> Veronica

The ancient chronicle of Japan, the *Kojiki*, describes Amaterasu Ōmikami vividly, just as if she were a character in a drama. She was descended from Izanaginomikoto, who went down to seek his dead wife to the land of Hades, where ugly maggots were creeping across her rotten body. Returning from this dark and dirty world, Izanagi made purification at *Tsukushi no tachibanano odono Awakihara* and then begot three noble children: Amaterasu Ōmikami, Tsukiyominomikoto, and Susanoonomikoto. Amaterasu was very beautiful from the moment of her birth, but her younger brother, Susanoo, was naughty as a boy; very sad because his mother had passed away, he did not stop weeping, and so Amaterasu scolded him. This realistic scene, one of family troubles, is readily understandable. Later Susanoo did not fulfill his duty of keeping the land peaceful and broke down the levees of Amaterasu's rice fields, filled in her irrigation ditches, and defecated in her palace. But she did not reproach him; instead she interpreted his conduct in a favorable light, and was very kind to him. Her name is often translated into English as the Sun Goddess. This is as eulogistic as the Japanese name Amatersasu Ōmikami is, and both are liable to be misconstrued as an astronomical star. But the real Amaterasu is not only a divine being and but also a human one. She did not have to be taught "benevolence," since she was very benevolent, tolerant and beautiful by nature. So it is believed that when human beings become as benevolent as her, they will become shiningly beautiful. Ancient people took this transfiguration realistically, as we can see in the *Kojiki* (Chikuro Hiroike, *Ise Jingū, Hiroike Works*, vol. 4, pp. 71–72).

Amaterasu issued a Great Imperial Edict enjoining her grandson, Niniginomikoto, to govern *Ashiharano Nakakuni* (Japan) (*Kojiki*, vol. 48), one of the three strata of the world (the top one being the heavenly *Takagamahara* where the gods live, the middle stratum being the earthly *Toyoashiharano Nakatsukuni*, where human beings [the Japanese] live, and the lowest one being *Yominokuni*, Hades, the land of the dead). Amaterasu's Great Imperial Edict established the national legitimacy of the government (see *CS* Chap. III, Sec. 1), and from Amaterasu and Niniginomikoto, the first Emperor, Jinmu, and 124 subsequent Emperors inherited the emperorship in succession mostly observing the *Daijousai* Rite, the Great Thanksgiving Festival.

So after Amaterasu's Edict successive Emperors and generations have faithfully followed its precepts for over 22 centuries. The original kings and leaders of nations or empires all reputedly hope for everlasting prosperity, but in reality all except the Japanese Imperial Family have failed to achieve this. Why? Any answer must incorporate the divine will evidenced in Amaterasu's Great Imperial Edict.

I cannot refrain from drawing attention to the significance of the fact that the Great Thanksgiving Service is conducted after the Enthronement. This is an important rite. The newly enthroned emperor eats rice with Amaterasu, which represents the transmission of Amaterasu's soul and implies that the new emperor shares her soul. This is indeed a mystic rite and is repeated at every enthronement.

The American writer, Nathaniel Hawthorne (1804–64), loved Italy, its history, its magnificent art treasures, and its architecture, as is clear in his fascinating romance *The Marble Faun* (1860). But in it the young American sculptor Kenyon also says to Donatello, the Count of Monte Beni, "You should go with me to my native country...In that fortunate land each generation has only its own sins and sorrows to bear." To this nineteenth century American, the Etruscans looked awfully old, older than the inhabitants of Rome itself, and he drew attention to the appearance of their "ponderous durability" (*Hawthorne's Works*, IV, 301). The remedy for this, in Hawthorne's words, was that "All towns should be made capable of purification by fire, or of decay within each half-century. Otherwise, they become the hereditary haunts of vermin and noisomeness; it seems as if all the weary and dreary Past were piled upon the back of the Present" (*Hawthorne's Works*, IV, 301–2). Similarly, in *The House of the Seven Gables*, Hawthorne writes that "It were better that they should crumble to ruin, once in twenty years, or thereabouts, as a hint to the people to examine into and reform the institutions which they symbolize" (*Hawthorne's Works*, II, 184). This twenty year period is exactly the same interval as that between each rebuilding (*Sengu*) of *Ise Jingū*, a practice which has been repeated for the past thirteen centuries, on a much larger scale and with a sincerer faith (Hawthorne could appreciate Shintō's sense of purity).

Sengu denotes the moving of the shrine where Amaterasu has been living to a new one in an alternate location every twenty years. The origin of this practice was Amaterasu's words to Yamatohime that Isenokuni, with its divine breezes, was the place where she wanted to live. She then moved from Yamato to Ise and settled there. Ise developed into a group of shrines: 32 thatched-roof shrines, 20 shingle-roofed shrines, and another four shingle-roofed shrines. The custom of *Sengu* was planned and institutionalized by the 40th Empress, Jitō. In her words, recorded in one ancient record puts it. "Spring has passed away, and summer seems to have come. The costume made of white cloth is dried on Heavenly Kaguyama" (*Mannyoushu* 1–28).

> 春過ぎて夏来るらし白たへの衣乾したり天の香具山
> （持統天皇万葉集 1–28）

So the Emperor and the people have carried out *Sengu* since A.D. 690, except for an interruption during the period of the civil wars. The present year, A.D. 2013, is that of the 62nd

Sengu, and once again Amaterasu has moved to a newly built shrine located next door to the old. The ceremony involves about 100 Shintō priests following with sacred music, and the Emperor who bows in the course of it.

Preparations for the ceremony are lengthy and involved, since it is not just a matter of constructing a new main shrine. This is, however, the central feature. Timber from more than 10,000 Japanese cypress trees is brought from the forests in the mountains of Kiso and Kii, and the surrounding areas in central Japan. It is felled between 100 and 200 years in advance of the preparations for the new shrine, because timber does not grow to a usable height and shape in just twenty years. In addition to tbe timber, many other things need to be made ready, including every detailed piece of the furnishings, the attire of the Shintō priests and of the workmen who contribute to this ceremony. The latter need to learn the techniques necessary to produce the replacement items, techniques that are passed down in an unbroken tradition fathers to sons. Special foods and dishes are also prepared by chefs, while the shrine whose life has ended, old pieces of furniture, and many others things are returned to the localities and used again. This is indeed an ecological approach and one that is very economical for those who are provided with such buildings.

Scores of important ceremonies, rituals and services are conducted for several years prior to the actual transfer of the shrine. Then the day of *Sengu*, literally the removal of a shrine, arrives, and Amaterasu Ōmikama moves from her old shrine to the new shrine, which symbolizes "evergreenness (*tokowaka*)." One of the most important rituals involved is the setting up of *Shinno mihashira* (the central pillar) which is buried underground at the center of the shrine at midnight, something not permitted to be seen by outsiders or described to them.

The central event in the ceremony itself is the moving of the Deity (Amaterasu) to the newly built shrine next door to the old one. 714 kinds of pieces are also moved, 1,576 items in all, including swords with jewels and various other furnishings and divine attire. The precincts are covered with white pebbles (*shiraishi*) brought to the site by over 206,000 devout people.

Apart from interruptions caused by civil wars, then, the ceremonies of *Sengu* have taken place continuously every 20 years since Empress Jitō's began the tradition in A.D. 690. The 62nd *Sengu*, celebrated in A.D. 2013, is another proof of the sincerity of the Japanese people that has been in evidence for the past thirteen centuries.

Bibliography

廣池千九郎『廣池博士全集』四「伊勢神宮と我国体」初版 1937, 第 2 版 1958

『日本書記』上, 坂本太郎・家永三郎・井上光貞・大野晋校注, 岩波書店, 1967, 1998

『古事記』口語訳, 三浦佑之, 文藝春秋, 2002

『古事記』山口佳紀・神野志隆光校注／訳, 小学館, 1997

『歴史読本―特集　伊勢神宮と出雲大社の謎』2013 年 6 月号, 中経出版

矢野憲一・篠原龍『伊勢神宮　日本人のこころのふるさとを訪ねて』講談社, 1991

櫻井勝之進『伊勢神宮』学生社, 1998

『歴史と旅　特別増刊 85　愛蔵版　百二十五代の天皇と皇后』秋田書店, 1997

『天皇 125 代』宝島社, 2014

Chapter IV

Two Civilizations and One City

Section 2

America: "An Enormous Laboratory" of Mankind

I.

Many thousands years ago in America, there were Pre-Columbia societies. People were from the outside. The settlers came from Asia to the American continent in three waves: the first wave in 13000 B.C. the second 7000 B.C. and the third in 2000 B.C. They had remained or have remained in primitive stages. Some of their ancestors who stayed in China, Korea, and Japan have developed into highly modernized societies. Their hereditary makings may be not greatly different, but the results are obvious. Primitive men were fit for primitive environments. Some of their faculties were more keen than those of modern men, much more sensitive in distinguishing faculties of colors, taste, sight, and medical cares. But after all, when primitive men encountered modern men, primitive men were to be defeated by them in the fields of immunity against diseases, military powers, and intelligence. When primitive societies meet with civilizations, alas, the former almost always faces defeat or even extinction.

II.

Then Europeans came to America in the 17th century seeking a "town on the hill" and the land of El Dorado respectively.

What is the Archetypal thinking of making America distinct from other nations or civilizations? Sacvan Bercovitch has made a great contribution in this field: that is typology. In his interpretation of types in the Bible, the incidents of the New Testament are predicted in the stories told in the Old Testament. For example, the fact that Jesus, in his infancy, escaped to Egypt (Matt. 2: 14) is predicted in the life of Moses who was, as an infant, divinely protected, and brought up in the Palace of Egypt. Another prefiguration is the story of Jonah: he was swallowed in a great fish or whale and stayed in it for three days and three nights, but he came out of it (Jonah 1–2). This is the prefiguration of the resurrection of Jesus after three days. Further, it is expanded to the idea that events after the New Testament will be predicted in the New Testament and the Old Testament. Further again, it is expanded to the idea that events told in the New Testament and the Old Testament will predict things in later periods. Therefore, the believers of this typology or a Biblical view of History try to realize these ideas. America was discovered by Columbus in 1492, and Martin Luther's Reformation was in 1517. The Revelation of John (7: 1) states it "the four corners of the earth," over which Christianity would spread. Until that time Christianity had spread to Africa, Europe and Asia. American Puritans wondered what the remaining one corner of the earth was. They believed it was American continent, which had been preserved sinless by the Providence.

So they decided to go to America. Here a famous dichotomy was born. Europe is the land of experience i.e. Old Adam after the Fall, America is the land of innocence i.e. Young Adam before the Fall. Here we can see the Archetypal Framework of American history. This is the Myth of America, and the American tradition.

The Pilgrim Fathers came across the Atlantic Ocean arriving at Plymouth in 1620. In *Of Plymouth Plantation*, William Bradford writes as follows:

> "Besides, what could they see but a hideous and desolate wilderness, full of wild beasts and wild men—and what multitudes there might be of them they knew not. Neither could they, as it were, go up to the top of Pisgah to view from this wildness a more goodly country to feed their hopes; for which way soever they turned their eyes (save upward to the heavens) they could have little solace or content in respect of any outward objects.... If they looked behind them, there was mighty ocean which they had passed and now as a main bar and gulf to separate them from all the civil parts of the world."

From Mount Pisgah in Palestine, Moses saw the Promised Land (Deuteronomy xxxiv: 1–4). It is very clear that in Bradford's mind, there was Moses' image crossing the Red Sea nearly three thousand years before him. To build a "city on the hill" was the idea of Bradford and his group. Was this dream of Utopia fulfilled? What they found here at the supposedly promised land was, as Hawthorne writes in his *The Scarlet Letter*, "the black flower of civilized society, a prison (CE 1: 48)" and cemetery.

Next John Winthrop came to Boston with thousan ͻ in 1630. They were Puritans. They were the forefaͭ ͍ers of modern Americans. That America had no ancient times, medieval ages nor feudal regime. They were modern people. The Europe that they left was the lands of kings and the Catholic authority. They wanted to have freedom and individualism. They set up the great spiritual foundation and archetype in America.

Let us review American history briefly.

III. An ideal to seek freedom and independence

1607		Plantation of Jamestown
1619		Plantation of Virginia. 20 black slaves were sold from a Dutch ship. Beginning of slavery
1620		Pilgrim Fathers' Plantation of Plymouth
1770	3/5	The Boston Massacre
1773	12/16	The Boston Tea Party
1774	4/19	Lexington-Concord. Start of the War of Independence
1775		"By the rude bridge that arched the flood, Their flag to April's breeze unfurled, Here once the embattled farmers stood And fired the shot heard round the world." (R. W. Emerson "Concord Hymn") Even Toynbee praises this poem in his essay of American Independence.
1776	7/4	The Declaration of Independence Emerson, "The American Scholar," 1837 Holmes's *obiter dictum*, "Our intellectual Declaration of Independence." The relation to Europe: Henry James, T. S. Eliot, and Ezra Pound suffered from European Virus

IV. America: A Nation of Immigrants, A Continental Nation of diverse races, cultures, and geographical features

In 1770–75, St. Jean de Crèvecoeur wrote in his *Letters from an American Farmer*,

"What then is the American, this new man? He is either an European, or the descendant of an European, hence that strange mixture of blood, which you will find in no other country. I could point out to you a family whose grandfather was an Englishman, whose wife was Dutch, whose son married a French woman, and whose present four sons have now four wives of different nations.... Here individuals of all nations are melted into a new race of men, whose labours and posterity will one day cause great changes in the world." *The American Tradition in Literature*, eds. Sculley Bradley, etc. (Grosset & Dunlap, 1974), 4th ed. 2 Vols, 1st vol., p. 184.)

Samuel Huntington writes,

"In the late nineteenth century, Americans increasingly defined themselves racially. This was most obvious with respect to Blacks and Asians, but white Americans also viewed Irish, Italian, Slavic and Jewish immigrants as racially different from themselves. As the generations passed and assimilation proceeded, the descendants of these immigrants came to be accepted as white Americans."

This self-question has been recurrently asked for the past

three centuries: Samuel P. Huntington's brilliant recent book, *Who Are We?*, 2004, after experiencing great changes of "The slow blurring of racial distinction and the fading salience of racial identities" (p. 295) or "The virtual disappearance of ethnicity as a source of identity for white Americans" (p. 295), still the fact of a complex fate remains. As time goes on, the degree of intermarriage in America proceeds to the following case:

> "In Family A, a Jewish-American marries a native of Korea. Their son married an immigrant who is 100 present Iranian. In terms of ancestry, the children of that marriage are one-quarter Jewish, one-quarter Korean, and one-half Iranian. In Family B, two-native born-American marries, one of pure-Armenian ancestry and one of pure Irish ancestry. Their daughter marries an immigrant who is 100 percent Egyptian. The child of that marriage thus one-quarter Armenian, one-quarter Irish, and one-half Egyptian. The third generation in each family has three very different ethnic ancestries. What would then happen if members of the third generation in each family married each other? The offspring of that marriage would one-quarter Iranian one-quarter Egyptian one-eighth Armenian one-eighth Irish, one-eighth Jewish, and one-eighth Korean" (p. 299).

When it happens, Huntington writes, "White America is changing from a multiethnic society of a few dozen ethnic groups into a no ethnic society of tens of millions of multiethnic individual" (p. 299).

Bibby writes, "the United States is culturally diverse, but there has been a historical sense that people who come to

America become Americans, regardless of how much they may value the cultures of their homelands" (p. 11).

This kind of American myth has been repeatedly expressed in novels and movies such as Faulkner's *Light in August* (Penguin Modern Classics, pp. 338–339) and "Anchor Woman." The former case is the story of a young man named Percy Grimm, a fanatic believer of Myth of America: "a sublime and implicit faith in physical courage and blind obedience, and a belief that the white race is superior to any and all other races and that the American is superior to all other white races and that the American uniform is superior to all men, and that all would ever be required of him in payment for this belief, this privilege, would be his own life" (p. 339). Of course such a man should be enlightened. The latter case is more pathetic. A few refuges on a small boat escaped from Cuba 25 feet before Miami Beach, almost arriving at the foaming American shore but expired. They believed in stepping on a promised land, the anchor woman reported. This is only one scene in that film, but memorable one.

Another case is not fictional but historical: the case of Brigham Young and his Mormon followers. They escaped from New York, walking to the West, crossing the Mississippi. At that time in their mind there was supposed to be an image of Moses crossing the Red Sea.

The Myth of America will appear again and again even in future time like this: Stephen Blaha writes: "To some extent we are in a situation similar to the beginning of the exploration of the Americas. We can choose a large-scale movement into space as Europe did with the Americas, or we can be content with communications/weather satellites and science-oriented space stations—and a limited global environment" (p. 208).

A Unified Quantitative Theory of Civilizations and Societies

9600 BC–2100 AD (Pingree-Hill Research Monograph Publishing, NH, 2005).

V. Seeking True Self before the birth of one's parents

Nathaniel Hawthorne's first American ancestor, William Hathorne came from England in 1630 with John Winthrop. The author is the 6th descendant and no relations with other racial ancestors. He was dispatched to Liverpool in England as American Consul in Liverpool, stayed there from 1853 to 57, and went to Europe, mainly to Italy, and back to England and to the United States in 1860 on the eve of the Civil War. During his stay in his ancestral country, England, he was always yearning after his ancestors. It is frankly described in *The English Notebooks,* and *Our Old Home.* One of the passages from *The English Notebooks* says as follows:

> "My ancestor left England in 1630. I return in 1853. I sometimes feel as if I had been absent these two hundred and eighteen years [223 years] leaving England just emerging from the feudal system, and finding it on the verge of Republicanism. It brings the two far separated points of time very closely together, to view the matter thus" (CE 21: 138).

He passed away in 1864. In October, 1868, four years after Hawthorne's death, Sophia, Una, Julian, and Rose left the Wayside, Concord, for Dresden, Germany, and in 1870, they moved to London. Sophia died in March 1871 in London, and Una died unmarried there in 1877. Rose entered the Catholic Church and became Mother Alphonsa and worked in New York. Recently bones of Sophia and Una were reburied from London to Concord, Massachusetts where Nathaniel Hawthorne was buried. In the case of the Hawthornes, no racial mixture I found, but because of his European experience he became a kind of "divided self."

A few decades later than Hawthorne, Henry James had more complex environments.

"It's a complex fate, being an American" (*Letters* I, 274), Henry James (1843–1916) once wrote. His grandfather was the second wealthiest Irish businessman in New York, his father a Swedenborgian theologian, his elder brother a philosopher William James. He has no biological complexity, as we quoted Huntington's *Who Are We?* (p. 299), but he was educated privately by tutors in various parts of Europe and the United States. He entered Harvard law school in 1862. He was so cosmopolitan in that he was suffering from "European virus." He could not find a home in America. He became naturalized in Britain in 1915. Though born in St. Louis, Mo., T. S. Eliot also naturalized in Britain, and Ezra Pound chose the life of expatriation.

VI.

Though Pound translated *Confucian Analects,* he did not followed the ways of socialization of the Confucian morals. In *The Cantos* and others, however, he succeeded in permeating the spirits of Confucius. T. S. Eliot followed Pound's advice of cutting and concentrating *The Waste Land*. The World War I looked to be the devastation of Western civilization. And so he wrote *The Waste Land:*

> What is the city over the mountains
> Cracks and reforms and bursts in the violet air

Falling towers
Jerusalem Athens Alexandria
Vienna London
Unreal

The last two lines are:

Datta. Dayadhvam. damyata.
   Shantih shantih shantih.

Shantih is, according to Eliot's note, the Peace which passeth understanding. In order to make our civilizations more peaceful, the teachings of the world sages are essential.

Chapter IV

Two Civilizations and One City

Section 3

A Glimpse of China: Past, Present, and Future

Chinese civilization is not only one of the oldest civilizations in the world but also still one of the major living civilizations. As is always the case of any living things on earth, civilizations are not exceptions. Why was China able to enjoy such an extended longevity as a civilization?

Chinese pseudo-history started in the time of the five emperors whom Si Ma Qian (c. 145–86 B.C.), a great Chinese historian of the Han Dynasty, described in detail. Confucius (551–479 B.C.) himself a historical researcher, however, took a more deliberate attitude towards legendary records, and selected only Yao and Shun, the last two, among the five emperors. Yao was renowned as a sage emperor, and his minister Shun was famous for his filial conducts to his wicked father. Shun married to Yao's daughter. Because Yao's son was not good enough, Shun succeeded to the throne. In those days, floods were rampant, and Shun ordered his minister Yu to control the floods. Before Yu, his father Gun had been punished due to his failure. Yu therefore worked very hard, concentrating his mind on the work, and for thirteen years he never rested at home, even when he passed by his own house. He had only simple clothes and meals, ...He kept his house and rooms humble and spent the money thereby saved to construct ditches and water-channels between fields."[1]

Shun's son was not good enough to be the emperor, and so Shun gave the throne to Yu. Yu's son was very good, and so Yu gave the throne to his son, and consequently Yu created the first dynasty called the Hsia, which existed between the dates of 2205–1766 B.C. (or 1994–1523 B.C.). Yu's great virtue, however, did not continue for long. The last king of the Hsia Dynasty was called Jie, a Nero-like wicked king, who was expelled from the throne by Tang.

The First Rebellion in China

Shang Shu, The book of Shang, The Announcement of Zhong Hui, states the following:

> "King Tang had Jie banished to Nan chao and felt ashamed of his conduct. He said: "I fear men in the future may use it as a pretext." Zhang Hui [King Tang's minister] then composed a statement which said, "...the king of Xia was behaved outrageously, people fell into distressed as if being pitched and burnt.... Once the lord of Ge killed the carrier of sacred food; so your first punishment was to Ge. When you [king Tang] went to the east, the western tribes complained, and when you went to the south, the northern tribes grumble. They said: "Why are we behind?" Wherever you went, all the families of the place rejoiced, saying, 'we have waited for our lord. For when he comes we are revived.' In this way, people have held Shang in

high regard for a long time."[2]

The Chronicle of Chinese Dynasties
Xia Dynasty
Shang (yin) Western Chou   1122 or 1027–770 B.C.
Eastern Chou (Spring and Autumn)   722–481 B.C.
Warring States   403–221 B.C.
Ch'in   221–206 B.C.
Former Han   202 B.C.–8 A.D.
Hsin   8 A.D.–25 A.D.
Later Han   25–220 A.D.
Three Kingdoms   220–280
Western Chin   265–317
Chin (Sixteen Kingdoms)   317–439
Liu Sung   420–479
Liang   502–557
Ch'en   557–589
Sui   581–618
T'ang   618–907
Five Dynasties and Ten Kingdoms   907–979
Sung   979–1126
Mongols   1271–1279
Yuan   1279–1368
Ming   1368–1644
Ch'ing   1644–1912

Kuomintang   1912–1949
People's Republic   1949–

The Formidable Assimilating Power of the Han (Chinese) Characters

The Chinese people consists of 56 tribes, of which the main

tribe is the Han Chinese.

In the long four thousand years of Chinese history, the first universal state (which is Toynbee's terminology) is the Chin-Han Empire (Former Han, 206 B.C.–A.D. 8; Later Han, 25–220), and Han set the standard or the basic framework as a Civilization, Confucianism, Taoism, and Buddhism spread.

Chinese Traditional View of their Surrounding Barbarians

The pivotal parts of China, mainly composed of the Han tribes, enjoyed prosperity; however, they had to be cautious of the barbarians' invasion. In order to do so, they had to keep building the Great Wall of China since the time of "Spring and Autumn" (722–481 B.C.), and "Warring States" (403–221 B.C.) on the northern border of China from the east to the west. Finally the Wall reached a length of 2400 kilometers.

Shi Huang-ti (259–210 B.C.) greatly enlarged it. Successive Chinese leaders had to defend themselves against the northern barbarians. For example, in the time of Wu Ti (141–87 B.C.) in Han Dynasty, the expeditions led by Wei Qing and Huo Qu-bing (140?–117 B.C.) went out of the Great Wall to fight against the northern tribes. In these periods the Han administration attempted to make amity by giving Hsiung-nu a beautiful Chinese princess named Wang Zhao-jun in 33 B.C. This is one example of placatory conduct. For many centuries, the central administration of China had to take a set of policies, which combine a hard and soft approach to the pastoral tribes, but eventually barbarians succeeded in occupying the main part of China. The two conspicuous cases are Mongol (Yuan) Dynasty (1271–1368) and Manchurian Qing Dynasty (1616–1912). The conquering Mongol rulers and their people became Sinicized, though in social classes the Mongols were on top, the second were the peoples from Uighur, the Tanguts, Persia, Arabs, and sometimes Europeans. And the third was the Han race.

Ming China

Of all the civilizations of premodern times, none appeared more advanced, none felt more superior, than that of China. Its considerable population, 100–130 million compared with Europe's 50–55 million in the fifteenth century; its remarkable culture; ...and its unified, hierarchic administration run by a well-educated Confucian bureaucracy had given a coherence and sophistication to Chinese society..."[3)]

Emperor Yongle (1360–1424) Appointed Cheng Ho to be the Admiral.

The most famous of the official overseas expeditions were the seven long-distance cruises undertaken by the admiral Cheng Ho (1371?–1435?) between 1405 and 1433.[4)] "Consisting on occasions of hundreds of ships and tens of thousands of men, these fleets visited ports from Malacca and Ceylon to the Red Sea entrances and Zanzibar... (It must be noted, ...that the Chinese apparently never plundered nor murdered—unlike the Portuguese, Dutch, and other European invaders of the Indian Ocean.)...

But the Chinese expedition of 1433 was the last of the line, and three years later an imperial edict banned the construction of seagoing ships; later still, a specific order forbade the existence of ships with more than two masts.... There was, to be sure, a plausible strategical reason for this decision. The northern frontiers were again under some pressure from the Mongols, and it may have seemed prudent to concentrate military resources in this more vulnerable area."[5)]

In the end of the Ming Dynasty, the greatest Jesuit missionary, Matteo Ricci (Chinese name, Li Ma-tou; 1552–1610) was sent to China in 1582. He was a really marvelous man: he was well-versed in prisms, clocks, geographic knowledge of "the world map" of 1602, as well as Mandarin, and literate in the Chinese classics. His contemporary Chinese were of course amazed at his great talent; however, they were slow or ignorant to realize the rise of the West, a completely different civilization, from the supposedly barbarian place of the earth.[6]

The causes of decline of Ming Dynasty were at first internal: effete rulers, factional jealousies among officials, and fiscal bankruptcy.

Ch'ing Dynasty

"Barbarian" invaders founded the Ch'ing Dynasty. But the Manchu conquerors preserved and used the major institutions of government that had fanctioned for more than two centuries under the Ming. The invaders thoroughly Sinicized in Qing Dynasty; typical examples are found in the personalities of two great emperors of this Manchu Dynasty: Kang-xi-di and Qian-long-di.

The fourth emperor Kang-xi-di (1654–1722) and the 6th emperor Qian-long-di (1711–1799) of the Qing Dynasty, both of whom were from non-Han race, were both well versed in the Chinese classics. The former made the famous *K'ang-hsi Dictionary*. He supported a massive encyclopedia, *Synthesis of Books and Illustrations of Ancient and Modern Times*, which is a good deal larger than the *Encyclopedia Britannica*.[7]

Qian-long-di Sinicized the Manchurian Emperor even more. He is said to have made nearly fifty thousand Chinese poems during his lifetime.

Kao-cheng-hsueh, the study of historical artifacts, was developed in the period of Ch'ing Dynasty. This method of study was effective in finding authentic texts and expelling forged ones. Once a certain value was established in the past text, it continues to be respected. Their ideal models were far in the past. The value is in the past, not in the present nor future. This attitude brings its society both stability, and stagnation. In the rapidly changing society, this attitude is not able to respond to new environments and consequently falls into decline. China did not experience dynamic social changes such as modern Europe experienced by the Renaissance, the Reformation, the Scientific Revolution, the French Revolution, and the Industrial Revolution. They were able to enjoy long peace under the Ming Dynasty (1368–1662) and the alien Ch'ing Dynasty (1644–1912).

Ke-ju, the Chinese civil service, recruited by public examination, was the longest-lived and most efficient example of an imperial administration. It started in Sui period in the 6th century and ended in 1905 in the Qing dynasty. There were three main levels of examination, and contents were Chinese classics, such as the *Great Learning, Golden Mean, the Analects of Confucius, Mencius*. And *the Five Classics of Confucianism: the Book of Change, the Book of History, the Book of Poetry, the Spring and Autumn Annals, and the Book of Rites*. Learning these Confucian classics by heart was effective to preserve the past system, but it was not fit for finding new discoveries and creativeness.

Toynbee writes in his *Survey of International Affairs, 1926*:

"The Chinese would not face the fact that, unknown to them, a civilization had arisen in the West which was entitled to rank with the Confucian culture, and that the representatives of this civilization could not with impunity be treated as barbarians. The Chinese stiffened their necks and paid the same penalty as the Persians paid when they encountered the Greeks, or the Byzantines when they encountered the crusaders.[8]

Westerners were treated as barbarians. For example, the Emperor Ch'ing Lung received Lord Macartney's embassy in 1793. The mission was one of several unsuccessful demonstrations of Western power. Traditionally they looked down their surrounding areas, by calling them eastern, western, northern, and southern barbarians. The etymology of the barbarian comes from the Greek, *bárbaros* one who speaks an unintelligible language. This attitude of *hubris* is very common among strong and hegemonic civilizations in the world. *Hubris* invites, however, penalty of nemesis.

The spirit of the comparative study of civilizations is to have a fair-minded, comprehensive view of the civilizations and encourage mutual learning and respect and self-examination.

Now in 2007, China launched into the new age of space competition as well as having big environmental problems. We earnestly hope China shall be open-minded and cooperative in the advancement of welfare and security of world peace.

Chapter IV

Two Civilizations and One City

Section 4

St. Petersburg Viewed from Comparative Civilizations

We are happy to know that St. Petersburg is now in 2003 celebrating its 300th anniversary since Peter the Great built the city for the purposes of defending the new Russia and opening a "window looking on Europe." It is both the military and cultural symbol of Russia.

In order to obtain a wider perspective, it is necessary to take into account geopolitical and historical considerations. Russia developed as time passed from the western part, somewhere near Novgorod to the eastern tips of Eurasia; the direction of its development is just the opposite of that of the United States. It now extends over eleven different time zones, and St. Petersburg is located on the western tip of Russia.[1]

We want to know the origin of Russia. It is not clear, however, obstructed by the haze of time. The first historical document in Russian history is in *The Primary Chronicle*, which was written in 1110 or 1112. It records a tribe called the

Varagians who, as one of the wandering tribes in the Scandinavian Peninsula, came into the western part of Russia in the ninth century. In the beginning, the Scandinavian element was strong. Sometimes the issue whether Russia belongs to Europe or Asia arises, but it is very clear that from the beginning to the time when Asia elements were added by the Mongolian invasion, Russia was European. In 862 Rurik, the founder of new dynasty, became prince of Novgorod.

Vladimir (c. 980–1015) married Anna, sister of the Byzantine emperor, and consequently he adopted Christianity in 988, through which formal culture came to Rus, an almost intellectually virgin territory, where there were no native religious or philosophical traditions vital enough to force a confrontation or synthesis such as occurred elsewhere. It was an epoch-making incident in Russian history. The Tartars came to Russia in 1223. Their manner of invasion was notorious in its atrocity, but their attitude to religions in Asian countries was generous, or lenient. They adopted Islam. Russia ceased to be simply European, but the spiritual backbone of Russia remained Greek Orthodox.

The defeat of Constantinople by the Turks in 1453 strengthened Russian confidence in Russian Orthodoxy.

The monk, Theophilus of Pskov, wrote an open letter addressed to the Grand Duke Basil III of Moscow:

> The Church of Old Rome fell because of its heresy; the gates of the Second Rome, Constantinople, have been hewn down by the axes of the infidel Turks; but the Church of Moscow, the Church of the New Rome, shines brighter than the Sun in the Universe.... Two Romes have fallen, but the Third stands fast; a fourth there cannot be.[2]

This letter declared that Russia took over the traditional Byzantine attitude towards the West, and this attitude continued not only up unto the Revolution of 1917 but also after it. Thus Russia claimed clearly that they are an inheritor of Byzantine civilization, and its religion became a spiritual anchor of the Russian people. The Bible was translated into the Slavic language. Its doctrine was accepted as perfect because at that time the orthodoxy-heterodoxy controversy was over. Therefore, neither study nor debate was encouraged, but faithful observance of the rituals was forced, leading to illiteracy and ignorance. Thus ritual became the core of Russian religion. From today's point of view, it is obvious that its religion proved to be a hindrance to modernization. Russians were usually forbidden to travel abroad, and the Russian Church strongly opposed any learning that detracted from religious worship. Secular knowledge was regarded as equivalent to heresy, arithmetic and geometry were treated as magic arts, and science generally was seen as the work of the Antichrist.

Russia was rather backward in comparison with more advanced Europe; so she desperately needed new knowledge and skills. For example, at the Court of Alexis (1645–1676), many foreigners were invited to live in rigidly segregated areas of Moscow. About 1672 (the year of Peter the Great's birth), some 18,000 foreigners were estimated to reside in the Muscovite empire. When they were introduced before the tsar, he performed a ritual ablution to cleanse himself of contamination.

Although similar segregation existed in Japanese history, it was not because of religious heresy but to prevent a political threat to national independence.

A big change of policy came from a casual chat by a Portuguese pilot with Japanese interlocutors. Toynbee writes:

"As early as A.D. 1596 the Japanese had been put on their guard against Spanish imperialism by some unwary remarks from the lips of the pilot-major of a wrecked Spanish ship, the *San Felipe*. In explanation of the enormous extent of the Spanish Crown's possessions as displayed on a map of the World which he had shown to his Japanese interlocutors with an eye to overawing them the imprudent Spaniard had declared that Spain's first move towards getting possession of any non-Western country on which she had political designs was to send missionaries to promote the formation of a native Christian party there which would serve, when the time came, as a spear-head for Spanish aggression (Boxer, *op. cit.*, pp. 165–166).... The Japanese political authorities' chief misgiving about Christianity and this misgiving was felt by the daimyo as well as the Bakufu—was that its claim in the allegiance of its Japanese converts might be a challenge to the claims of feudal loyalty...."[3]

"Before his death in 1598 Hideyoshi had became distrustful of the Christian missionaries, particularly the Portuguese, and Ieyasu, too, seems finally to have concluded that loyalty to Edo, as he thought of it, was incompatible with loyalty to Rome, as he understood that.[4] Since then, the Tokugawa Bakufu created a policy to expel most missionaries, especially after the massive rebellion caused by supposedly Christian samurais and peasants on the Shimabara peninsula in 1637–38."

In the case of Russia during the Reign of Alexis (1645–1675), Western science and thought were regarded as anti-Christ and heresy[5]: this case is within the same Christian civilization. The issue was a religious and cultural matter, but in the case of Japan, the issue was an encounter between two different civilizations: and it was not a matter of heresy but the matter of loyalty to a feudal daimyo and finally national independence.

Then only the Dutch were permitted to keep a small trading port at Deshima (1641–1859), a water-girt depot in Nagasaki.

Thomas Garrigue Masaryk (1850–1938) writes in his Preface to *The Spirit of Russia*, "Russia is clearly divided into two: i.e. the old Russia before Peter the Great and Russia after him."[6]

Devoted but not enlightened was the intellectual atmosphere when Peter the Great appeared in Russian history. He was a real genius: he went to Europe and stayed a year and a half (1697–98) visiting Holland, England, and other countries, and he mastered 18 different skills including shipbuilding. He brought back his new knowledge to Russia. His fighting against the Old Believers and boyars is famous or infamous as Antichrist activities. Education by force was the keynote of Petrine educational policy. The Old Believer's beards were forcibly shorn in Peter the Great's campaign to Westernize Russian life and manners.

Objectively, Russia became a peripheral civilization to the Byzantine civilization; however, it seems to have become independent from Byzantium from the middle of the 15th to the middle of the 16th century. Now at the time of Peter the Great, Russia became a peripheral civilization to the West.

When two civilizations, one major and aggressive, the other peripheral and passive, meet, three kinds of responses arise on the side of peripheral civilization:

Toynbee's analysis of this situation in the following terms is very useful:
1. Zealotism—nationalistic, traditional, expelling foreign influences;
2. Herodianism—learning excellent things even from foreign countries, and wanting to strengthen his own country;

3. Evangelism—Jesus Christ's way of life.

Toynbee aptly describes the two opposing groups as Zealotians and Herodians. They took "the opposing attitudes towards Hellenism, and contrary policies for coping with it, of two Jewish parties in the Palestinian province of the Syriac World in the time of Christ that appear in the New Testament under the names of 'Zealots' and 'Herodians'."[7] To the overwhelming Hellenistic culture, these Zealots tried to defend themselves by retreating into "the spiritual fortress of their own Jewish heritage, lock themselves up within this psychic *donjon*, close their ranks, maintain an unbroken and unbending front, and find their inspiration, their ideal, and their acid test in the loyalty and sincerity of their observance of every jot and tittle of a traditional Jewish law."[8]

This attitude of Zealotianism is being unable to see the progress of science and thought and consequently subject to defeat by overwhelming enemies.

On the contrary "the anti-Zealot Herodian faction was recruited from the servants, supporters, and admirers of an opportunist statesman," King Herod. He took "a fresher and less prejudiced view of jewry's Hellenic problem than was opened to contemporary Judean Jews."[9]

The Islamic Afghanistan's response to the West in 1929 was apparently Herodian but in essence a Zealotian mind. This is very instructive.

> "On the 27th November, 1929, King Nadia of Afghanistan published a declaration of policy in ten points: first, the foundation of his government upon the principles of Islamic Law; the second, the absolute prohibition of alcoholic beverages; the third, the establishment of a military school and of an arsenal for the manufacture of

modern weapons; ...the eighth, the development of commercial relations with foreign powers; the ninth, the advancement of public instruction; ..."[10]

Some of the above ten points try to keep people within the Islamic enclosure; however, the ninth allows people to be influenced by Western thoughts. This is unavoidable. The third is also vulnerable to being affected by Western technology, or rather they seemed to intend, implicitly or explicitly, to learn Western technology. In the year 1929, a certain religious authority was reported to have exhorted Afghan students "to study the Occidental as well as the Oriental sciences, on the ground that all sciences are useful, being light from the lights of God." He further exhorted them to learn foreign languages in order to equip themselves for frustrating the knavish tricks of foreign enemies.... We may read between the lines that he was willing to sanction the study of the Satanic sciences of the West because he realized that this was the only means by which an Islamic community in his generation could avert the greater evil of falling under the economic and political ascendancy of the Westerners.[11]

Toynbee drew this conclusion concerning the Herodian response to the stronger civilizations:

"...yet, when the Zealots of Islam themselves adopted the Herodian tactics of fighting the West with its own weapons, it was evident that the days of Zealotism in the Islamic World were numbered even in its last strongholds."[12]

When we consider Peter the Great's and subsequent Russian responses to the West, we can easily find similar responses from the peripheral civilizations. There are several major civilizations such as Greece, India, China, Islam, the West, etc, and their correspondent peripheral civilizations. Many studies could be made in this field.

Peter the Great had to reform both foreign and domestic affairs, which had been stiffened under the influences of his contemporary Greek Orthodoxy: it was strongly ritualistic, mysticism-oriented, and not morality-oriented. It was Peter the Great's task to build a strong Russia and catch up with the European levels in all aspects of life. In order to do so, he ordered his people to build schools, to translate Western books into Russian, to introduce mathematics, mechanical engineering, physics, chemistry, and other natural sciences, which had been formerly regarded as "magic art" upon whose principles cannons, battleships, fortress, fountains, city-planning, grand edifices were made.

A high spiritual tradition existed in Russian history. For example St. Antony (c. −1073) stayed in a cave for forty years, something like Saint Daniel the Stylite (409–93), not in a cave but on top of a pillar…The purpose of my mentioning such a spiritual leader is to respond to the third way of Evangelism by Toynbee. Pitirim Sorokin, as the first president of the International Society for the Comparative Study of Civilizations, wrote *Altruistic Love* (1950).[13] "According to him those called sages and saints, though having no wealth or power, had a decisive influence on the development of culture and social organizations and on the direction of history."[14]

Russia produced such distinguished comparative civilizationists as Nikolai Danilevskii (Russia I Everoa) and Pitirim Sorokin. The University of St. Petersburg produced such World figures as Ivan Pavlov, Aleksandr Pushkin, Pyodor Dostoyevsky, and Leo Tolstoy among many others.

Toynbee says, "in our present-day world it is imperative that different cultures shall not face each other in hostile competition, but shall seek to share their experience as they already share a common humanity."

During the past three centuries, the destiny of this beautiful city was not calm because of disturbances, revolution, war and siege; and its name changed several times: St. Petersburg, — Petrograd, Leningrad and then back to St. Petersburg. After World War I, experiencing the destruction of Europe, T. S. Eliot wrote *The Waste Land* (1922) envisioning the collapses of Judaic, Greek, Islamic, and contemporary European civilizations as follows:

What is the city over the mountains
Cracks and reforms and bursts in the violet air
Falling towers
Jerusalem Athens Alexandria
Vienna London
Unreal[15] (ll. 372–377)

Peter the Great built marvelous fountains in the city of St. Petersburg, utilizing the differences of the water levels, one of the evidences of his technological genius. Water is the symbol of eternal life. Yesterday we also visited the world famous museum, the Hermitage, which was built by Empress Catherine II, who was born a German princess, after she ascended the Russian throne. She brought in over three million pieces of European art. Thanks to Catherine the Great we can enjoy European culture here in Russia.

I pray from the bottom of my heart that St. Petersburg will be a window looking outo not only onto Europe but also the world in the spirit and respective of Comparative Civilizations.

Chapter V

The Civilizational Soul

Chapter V

The Civilizational Soul

Preamble

We have reached the final chapter of *the Civilizational Soul*. Then what is the Civilizatioal Soul in a word? Briefly, I will answer, it is the Supreme Morality, which is taught and practiced by the world sages. In the world, in the past and present, there are many problems in spite of many noble endeavors by the sages and conscientious peoples, still we have to solve many problems. In the preceding chapters I have discussed the vistas of the Comparative Study of Civilizations (chap. I), in which I explained an outlook of my interest.

What is the Civilizational Soul, more in detail, which is a new concept and a new expression? I believe each civilization has some hidden, or some times apparent ideal or kernel, though they are different each other in appearance, but in the behind idea, we can find common ideal: each civilization tries to attain a happy state of life. For these ideals the world sages and the founders of higher religions, which Hiroike and Toynbee mentions as the founders of Higher Religions of the world; five great sages, Amaterasu Ōmikami, Buddha, Confucius, Jesus Christ, Socrates, and some other sages, worked very hard.

The first stage of this chapter is to put Hiroike's moralogy in the history of the Western Moral Science and to clarify how moralogy is radically different, unprecedentedly different from hitherto Western moral science. The main purpose of Western moral science was to elucidate or analyze the moral or ethical terms minutely.

The second is the scope or width of collected materials. In the Western moral science, for example, James Beattie (1735–1803), a Scotch moral philosopher, in his *Elements of Moral Science* (1790–1793) gathered the materials from the Old and the New Testaments, Classical literature, Shakespeare, Milton (1608–74), Bishop Joseph Butler (1692–1752) and some other Western literary figures.

My humble attempt to write in *the Civilizational Soul* is, to catch a vision of "God revealing Himself in action to souls that were sincerely seeking Him. Since 'no man hath seen God at any time' and our clearest visions are but 'broken lights' of Him, there are as many angles of visions as there are vocations" (Toynbee, *A Study of History*, vol. X, 1), my humble vision of angle is a combination of my study of English and America literature, Comparative Study of Civilizations (mainly Arnold J. Toynbee), and two Japanese masters of civilizational soul, Hiroike Chikuro and Mori Ōgai, and finally *The Unprecedentedness of Moralogy Viewed from the History of Western Moral Science*.

Chapter V

The Civilizational Soul

Section 1

Introducing Moralogy: Bridging the East and the West

In this paper I would like to address the connection between moral science and the comparative study of civilizations. Because Chikuro Hiroike, the founder of Reitaku University, had a global view of civilizations, I thought it is appropriate for me as a Reitaku professor to introduce some of the founder's thoughts on moral science. Since the comparative study of civilizations is descriptive and explanatory as well as prescriptive and mission-oriented, Hiroike's moral science might be instructive in our study of civilizations.

At first, let us look at Hiroike's formative years of moral science. Previously, he had been well-known as a distinguished scholar of Japanese, Chinese, and Korean laws, histories, and languages, and a compiler of the *Kojiruien*, an encyclopedia of 51 volumes. It is said that he wrote over one fourth of the entries in the encyclopedia, which covers things Japanese from ancient times down to the 1860's. Many years of intensive study, however, ruined his health. At his worst, in December 1912, he was unable to eat, drink or see at all, and his doctors gave up all hope for him."[1] At that most critical time, he made a pledge to God to write a book about the enlightenment and salvation of mankind.

A few years before, he entered a Shintō faith, Tenrikyo, and he made a gift to it of his entire collection of books, some of them priceless, accumulated over twenty years. Meanwhile, he introduced some reforms and renovations, whose plans were eventually rejected, and he was forced to resigned. Now, when he left, he had "no money, no books, and no friend to turn to": all he had was "an enfeebled body, shattered by nervous collapse."

However, he never became bitter, or felt resentment against anyone. Instead, he turned his thoughts more deeply upon himself and laid all the blame on his own lack of virtue. With a grateful heart, he saw in his own condition an opportunity to verify his long-held belief that morality is the root of human life and happiness."[2] Then he began to formulate a system of moral science, later to be called moralogy, seeking truth through the uncharted seas of science, religion, and philosophy of the East and the West.

He called his scientific investigation of moralities moral science, following the examples of Western moral science. Gradually he found, however, his moral science very different from Western ones[3]; therefore he named his system *moralogy*, a newly coined word from Latin *moralis* plus Greek *-ology*. His ideas are captured in *A Treatise on Moral Science: A First Attempt at Establishing Moralogy as a New Science* (1928), a book about 3,500 pages in Japanese.

Hiroike's Moral Science Is Different from Western Moral Science as follows:

1. Take an example from Wayland's *The Elements of Moral Science*. This is "the science of human duty,"[4] extracted from passages of the Scriptures. He rejected utilitarianism and stated "the eternal validity of the moral law revealed in the Scriptures and man's consequent obligation to revere and worship the Divine Revealer."[5] Joseph L. Blau writes, "Wayland foresaw no possibility of a conflict of science and religion,"[6] however, in the middle of the nineteenth century, science had not been advanced enough to establish moral science in a positive way.
2. Leslie Stephen was well aware of the lack of well-advanced sciences, especially psychology, sociology, statistics, and political economy, when he wrote of the "Difficulty of Moral Science" in *The Science of Ethics* (1882).[7]
3. Taking into account the fact that Hiroike wrote his book several decades later than most Western moral scientists, he was able to adopt the fruits of more advanced natural, social, and human sciences available, and he stood in a more advantageous position, using advanced ideas with a wider perspective of the learning of the East and the West.
4. Moralogy resembles the comparative study of civilizations in an interdisciplinary sense. Hiroike formulated moralogy by using the following branches of science:
    a. The natural sciences:
    geology, physical geography, biology, the theory of evolution, genetics (including the theory of heredity), euthenics, eugenics, physiology, ethnogeny, archaeology,

b. The social sciences:
ethnography, anthropology, ethnology, Jurisprudence, psychology, sociology, criminology, the history of systems of law, the history of political economy, the history of morality.[8]

c. The humanities:
the history of civilizations (world history in general), Western philosophy, ethics, Christian theology/Studies of Buddhism, Confucianism, and Shintoism Japanese history, Chinese and Korean legal histories, Classical Chinese grammar.

5. The structure of moralogy is unique. Let me read the simplified contents of the *Treatise:* (its full contents run about 100 pages).

The Preface and the Three Introductions

Book One   A Scientific Investigations of the Principles and Practices of Traditional or Conventional Morality and of Supreme Morality

Chapter 1   What Is Moralogy? A Learning to demonstrate scientifically the effects of moral practice

Chapter 2   Moralogy and the Perfection of Human Life

Chapter 3   The Given Causes of Man's Division into Classes

Chapter 4   Acquired Causes in the Making of Human Classes

Chapter 5   The Fundamental Principle Concerning the Spiritual and Material Life of Mankind

Chapter 6   Observations on How Man's Past Mental Activity has Caused His Present Physique,

Chapter 7	Ways of Life and Future Destiny Investigations into Instinct, Knowledge, Morality, Social Constitution, the Nature of Civilization, the Happiness of Mankind, with Regard to Their Interrelations
Chapter 8	Observations on the Laws of Evolution and Degeneration of Mankind
Chapter 9	A. Errors in Modern Thought Concerning the Way of Realizing Universal Peace and Happiness B. Errors in the Policies and Methods Followed by Aristocrats, Multimillionaire, Capitalists and Landowners Concerning Labour Problems, Tenancy Disputes, National Enterprises of Public Welfare, Social Work or Charity Work
Chapter 10	Conventional or Ordinary Morality
Chapter 11	Tendencies of Civilizational Progress and Qualitative Progress of Morality
Chapter 12	Those who Have Practised Supreme Morality—Socrates, Jesus Christ, Buddha, Confucius
Chapter 13	A. The Sacred Virtue of Amaterasu Omikami who Laid the Foundation of Japan's Imperial House, and the Real Cause of the Unbroken Line of Succession of that House B. Investigations into the Causes of the Unbroken Lines of Succession of the Japanese Imperial House and Other Houses
Chapter 14	The Principles, Substance, and Content of

Supreme Morality
Chapter 15   The Effects of the Practice of Supreme Morality
Book Two   A Synopsis of Supreme Morality
Chapters 1–10

6. Advocating "Supreme morality"

Hiroike examined the thought and morality of the great sages, such as Buddha, Confucius, Jesus Christ, and Socrates, and found the commonalities among their thoughts and deeds and named their morality as "Supreme Morality." He expounded in detail the contents and the methods of the practice of supreme morality, and categorized it in the six principles as follows:

The Six Moral Principles
1. The Principle of the Renunciation of Self
2. God, or the Principle of benevolence
   Hiroike says, "benevolence includes an unbiased and universal love of humanity. Its application, then, must not be hampered by any distinction of race, nation, or religion."[9]
3. The Principle of the Precedence of Duty over Personal Rights
4. The Ortholinon Principle
5. The Principle of Human Enlightenment and Salvation
6. The Principle of Moral Causality

Any system of thought is a product of a particular historical time and place, people and climate, languages and symbols, etc. Bread and wine in Christianity, rice and *sake* in Japanese Shintoism are only a few examples which show how they are bound by particular environments. In a sense, Hiroike winnowed "the chaff away from the grain in Mankind's religious heritage,"[10] i.e. disengaged the essence from the nonessentials,[11] and found "supreme morality" or benevolence. (The fact that Hiroike expressed benevolence in Japanese, even if in any human language whatever, allows the creeping in of a particular bias, however small it may be. That is, however, inevitable, if the Universe is a mystery, and as St. Paul says, "For now we see in a mirror, dimly."[12] Another poetical explanation of the limitation of human ken is as follows:

> Buddha told his disciples what he thought they could understand and live up to. His teaching was not meant to be a full explanation of everything, a complete revelation of all that is. Once, it is said, he took some dry leaves in his hand and asked his favourite disciple, Ānanda, to tell him whether there were any other leaves besides those in his hand. Ānanda replied: 'The leaves of autumn are falling on all sides, and there are more of them than can be numbered.' Then said the Buddha: 'In like manner I have given you a handful of truths, but besides these there are many thousands of other truths, more than can be numbered.[13]

7. Hiroike's method: comparative, integrative, and convergent (on morality)

He attempted to demonstrate the practical value of supreme morality, comparing it with conventional morality and immorality: (1) from the perspective of the history of mankind; (2) from the sociological point of view; (3) through the selective inclusion of current scientific achievement; and also (4) on the basis of his own personal experience and observations. The purpose of moralogy is to demonstrate scientifically the effects of moral practices. Hiroike writes as follows:

> Now the main defect of traditional moral teaching lies in the argument that since the result of moral practices cannot be ascertained with any degrees of accuracy, the true value of morality can only be discerned in the goodness of the agent's motive, for the expectation of good results from moral practices is in itself an impure motive. If it were true that no good results can necessarily be expected from the practices of morality, then it would be impossible for most people to live a moral life without expectation of reward, except in the case of the 'Sages' themselves, or at the other extreme, of people whose psychology must be classed as abnormal.[14]

It does not mean, however, that moralogy is a system of utilitarian morality. On the contrary, it recommends us to practise the supreme morality practised by the great sages of the world. In moralogy, happiness is the result of the perfection of one's own moral character. But in the eudaemonistic ethics of all hedonism and utilitarianism, their direct targets are earthly happiness itself.[15]

Samuel P. Huntington's *The Clash of Civilizations and the Remaking of World Order* (not his article, "The Clash of Civilizations?" in *the Foreign Affairs*, Summer, 1993) is both descriptive (in his analysis of the Clash of Civilizations) and prescriptive (in his proposals of the Remaking of World Order). He is a realistic scholar of international politics, and strategist of writing scenarios of wars between China and the United States, wars among India, Pakistan, China, and Iran, war between Arab and Israel, and further the truly global civilizational war. Of course, he is not making fun of these bizarre scenarios. He proposed the *abstention rule* and the *joint mediation rule*, and the *commonalities rule* for the prevention of multicivilizational war. He writes as follows:

> At least at a basic "thin" morality level, some commonalties exist between Asia and the West. In addition, as many have pointed out, whatever the degree to which they divided humankind, the world's major religions—Western Christianity, Orthodoxy, Hinduism, Buddhism, Islam, Confucianism, Taoism, Judaism—also share key values in common. If humans are ever to develop a universal civilization, it will emerge gradually through the exploration and expansion of these commonalities....
>
> This effort would contribute not only to limiting the clash of civilizations but also to strengthening Civilization in the singular (hereafter capitalized for clarity). The singular Civilization presumably refers to a complex mix of higher levels of morality, religion, learning, art, philosophy, technology, material well-being, and probably other things.[16]

Huntington's proposal to seek commonalities shares similarities with Hiroike's finding supreme morality among the five moral systems. For the peaceful world, one should have one's particular faith, but should not bulldoze his or her own self-righteous "universalism" to others; rather, we should endeavor to seek and recreate commonalties among the best of civilizations.

There are nowadays very many corrupt practices among elite bureaucrats, businessmen, bankers, politicians, even children, as well as conflicts and wars. Parents and teachers, and the mass media are responsible for such social trends. Treaties, laws, regulations, and conferences are necessary. However, the most fundamental target to aim at is to eradicate our egotism, selfishness, egocentrism or whatever we want to call it. This is the perennial problem of humankind. The method of social reconstruction is rightly stated in the following classics:

> In very ancient times, those who desired to elucidate Supreme Virtue throughout the Empire, first had to establish good government within their own States, and, before they could do this, they had to regulate their own families harmoniously. This in turn called for the previous cultivation of their persons, which could only be accomplished by the rectification of their minds. To rectify their minds, they had first to have the will to be sincere; this desire could only be realized by the acquisition of knowledge. This acquisition of knowledge involved the investigation of all things, which in turn led to true knowledge. Having attained true knowledge, their will became sincere, and thus their minds were rectified. Possessing such superior minds, their persons became cultivated, and the regulation of their families became harmonious; their families being thus regulated, they governed their various states well, so that tranquillity and happiness prevailed throughout the Empire.[17]

Hiroike tried to present his moralogy as a protocol for world peace with all his sincerity and vital energy seventy years ago. As Ralph Waldo Emerson said in his *Self-Reliance*, "An institution is the lengthened shadow of one man." The present Institute of Moralogy and Reitaku University are the shadows of Dr. Chikuro Hiroike.

Chapter V

The Civilizational Soul

Section 2

For the Internationalization of Moralogy
A Tentaive Reply to Dr. Lauwerys' Proposals on National Ortholinon

I

Dr. Lauwerys, Mr. Chairman, members of the Institute and the University, and all other participants.

It is a great honour and privilege for me to speak before you on the internationalization of Moralogy.

The first substantial encounter between Moralogy (East) and West was made in a series of lectures by Dr. Joseph Lauwerys and related discussions with Japanese Moralogians on June 7, 8, 21, 22 and July 12, 1977.

During these meetings, especially in the last meeting, we found a very sincere and honest critic on the principle of national ortholinon in Dr. Lauwerys' character and erudition. He was brought up mainly in Western civilization, but has experienced world-wide educational activities. Moreover, he was the first foreign scholar who had really read or perused, at least, the part of moralogy concerned with the ortholinon principle. He was conscientious enough to read the English translation of the *Characteristics of Supreme Morality and Moralogy*, and no less than 500 typewritten pages from the *Treatise on Moral Science*, more than six times. It is quite natural, therefore, that his criticism and proposals for the internationalization of Moralogy should hit home and invite us to a new situation with which we could never be confronted in Japan. That is, what Dr. Lauwerys has tried to do is to make Moralogy in Japan applicable to the outside world or more specifically to Western society. This problem is, however, inherent in the essence of Moralogy, for Moralogy must be universal, not parochial, as a logical result of Moralogy as a science and for the ultimate purpose of Moralogy—the salvation of Mankind.

II

Such a task to make Moralogy in Japan applicable to Western society has many parallels in history. It does not matter whether Moralogy is a mental science, a philosophy, or a religion. If I am allowed to adopt Toynbee's terminology, Moralogy could be classified as a higher religion. When Moralogy is introduced to foreign countries, it will becme *a kind of* foreign mission, and there are many precedential cases of both success and failure in such foreign missions. It would, therefore, be useful for us to discuss some problems raised from foreign missions in general before we consider how to make Moralogy in Japan applicable to Western society.

Dr. Toynbee deals with this problem in Chapter 19, "The Task of Disengaging the Essence from the Non-Essentials in Mankind's Religious Heritage" in his *An Historian's Approach to Religion*.

To summarize this chapter, we get the following items:

1. "It is certain that any religious heritage, at any stage of

its history, will be compounded of essential elements [grain] and accidental accretions [chaff]..." (p. 270).[1] In other words, "[i]n the heritage of each of the higher religions we are aware of the presence of two kinds of ingredients. There are essential counsels and truths, and there are non-essential practices and propositions" (p. 262).

2. "These accidental accretions are the price that the permanently and universally vailed essence of a higher religion has to pay for communicating its message to the members of a particular society in a particular stage of this society's history...if the eternal voice did not 'tune in' to its present audience's receiving-set, its message would not be picked up. But, in order to be picked up, the message has to be denatured to some extent by a translation of what is permanent and universal into terms of something that is temporary and local...If the essence of a higher religion did not compromise with local and temporary circumstances by 'tuning in' to them, it would never reach any audience at all: ..." (p. 264).

3. When one tries to transplant a religion born in a certain civilization to another civilization, and to get convents, one needs to winnow the chaff from the grain, or to disengage the essence from the nonessentials in the religion.

4. "[Y]et the operation is always as hazardous as it is indispensable" (p. 270).

5. "Higher religions are historical institutions" (p. 263); if they could stand without any contact with other worlds, there would arise no problems. But it is impossible. They are now more urgently pressed to try to

disengage the essence from non-essential accretions than before because of the rapid change of time and of "'the annihilation of distance' through the achievements of a Late Modern Western technology has brought all the living higher religions, all over the World, into a much closer contact with one another than before" (p. 261). Each of the higher religions is required to re-examine its essence and accretions and to adjust itself to a new situation in a new Space-Time.

6. "For the distinction between the essence and the accidents in Religion in one which the ecclesiastical authorities, always and everywhere, are reluctant to admit" (p. 265). "One generic evil of an institution of any kind is that people who have identified themselves with it are prone to make an idol of it. The true purpose of an institution is simply to serve as a means for promoting the welfare of human beings...The responsible administrators of any institution are particularly prone to fall into the moral error of feeling it to be their paramount duty to preserve the existence of this institution of which they are trustees. Ecclesiastical authorities have been conspicuous sinners in this respect, though ecclesiastics have not been exceptionally sinful persons...Churches have been the most longlived and most widespread of all institutions hitherto known, and their unusual success as insitutions has made their institutional aspect loom unusually large in their official administrators' eyes" (p. 266). "Man's true end is to glorify God and to enjoy Him for ever; and, if the ecclesiastical authorities were to make this true purpose of their religion the paramount consideration in the determination of their

policy, they would be constantly re-tuning their unvarying essential message to different wave-lengths in order to make it audible to different audiences. Instead, they are apt to make the preservation of their church their paramount aim; and this consideration tempts them to insist that their religious heritage must be treated as an indivisible whole, in which the accidental accretions are to be accepted as being not less sacrosanct than the essence itself. They are moved to take this line by two fears. They are afraid of distressing and alienating the weaker brethren, and they are afraid that, if once they admit that any element in the heritage is local and temporary and therefore discardable, they may find themselves unable to draw a line or make a stand anywhere, till the very essence of the religion will have been surrendred" (pp. 266–267).

7. Toynbee has pointed out the following six non-essential accretions that can be, and ought to be, discarded: —
   a. The local holy places such as Heliopolis, Delphi, Jerusalem, Mecca, Bodh Gaya, Benares, Wu T'ai Shan.
   b. Rituals such as pilgrimages to holy places, the kissing of the toe of the bronze statue of St. Peter, the Passover, the Muslim's daily round of prayers, the Christian and the Mahayananian Buddhist liturgies.
   c. Tabus such as not to eat pork ever, not to eat the flesh of mammals on Fridays, not to work on the Sabbath and so on.
   d. Different social conventions: "celibacy versus marriage for a Christian priest according to the Latin as against the Eastern Orthodox rite;

monogamy for a Christian layman versus polygamy for a Muslim up to a limit of four wives; stringency versus laxity in the Christian as against the Muslim regulation of divorce, caste versus the brotherhood af all believers in the Hindu as against the Islamic or the Sikh Community" (p. 279).

e. Myths: "Though shrines, rituals, tabus, and social conventions are highly charged with feeling, they do not come so close to the heart of a religion as its myths, the portrayal of death as the seed of life in the figure of Tammuz-Adonis-Osiris-Attis, embodying the fruitfulness of the year that dies to be born again, the portrayal of selfsacrifice for the salvation of fellow-sufferers in the figure of Christ or of a bodhisattva...Can these myths be discarded without taking the heart out of the faiths whose essence the myths convey? If the Universe is a mystery, and if the key to this mystery is hidden, are not myths an indispensable means for expressing as much as we can express of the ineffable?...

This is true; and it does mean that myths are indispensable to Man for probing a mystery that is beyond his intellectual horizon. Yet no particular myths can be sacrosanct; for myths are woven out of poetic images borrowed from This World's passing scene... [and] the stuff of which myths are fashioned is mostly local and ephemeral" (p. 280).

In foreign missions, one must winnow these accidental accretions from the essence. In the history of Western missionaries of Christianity, the controversy between the Society of Jesus and the Franciscan and Dominican Orders gives us a good moral lesson.

Toynbee writes as follows:

"The Jesuits in the mission-field had been trying to divert Christianity of its Western accretions in order to make sure that the non-Christian audience to whom they were addressing their message should not be deterred from accepting the essence of Christianity through being required also to accept things whose association with it was merely local, temporary, and accidental. In this seventeenth-century 'Battle of the Rites', the Society of Jesus suffered defeat; but the experience of the following 250 years has been demonstrating, more and more conclusively, that the Jesuits were as rights as they were brave in resolutely wielding the winnowin-gfan" (p. 265).

From these previous discussions which Toynbee presents, we have been led to admit that in order to make moralogy in Japan applicable in Western society, we have to disengage the moralogical essence from nonessential accretions which are wearing, as it were, Japanese costumes. In other words, we have to strip moralogy of a local and temporary Japanese suit of clothes in order to reclothe it in an also local and temporary Western suit of clothes if we want moralogy to take root in the Western soil.

Toynbee's conclusion on this matter is, I believe, just compatible with Dr. Hiroike's attitude towards this matter. He writes of how to transplant the principle of ortholinon in foreign places:

"In supreme morality, therefore, instead of indoctrinating the authority of supreme morality in the inhabitants and worshippers, we should make more effort to increase spiritually and materially the happiness of the native inhabitants and visitors by adding authoriry to the god, the buddha, or the soul of the great man that has benefited them up to and since then. To exert this kind of effort is a true means of spreading the idea of the ortholinon conceived in supreme morality."[2]

He writes that "all conduct, to be moral, must be fitted to the circumstances, so the method of the conduct may vary, but the spirit of the conduct and the moral principle of practising it should always be the same."[3]

In the next section, let us search for a way for the application of the principle of national ortholinon to Western society, keeping in mind the essential spirit of supreme morality.

III

The principle of national ortholinon was formed by Dr. Chikuro Hiroike, whose major fields were Oriental law and history, in the ethos of the Meiji Constitution which had a strong emphasis on the Emperor's prerogative. Notwithstanding this, basic concept of the national ortholinon is broad enough to apply to many different countries, polities and nations. He writes as follows:

XIV. ix. 9.

Despite the Differences of the National Structure, Civil Polity and Racial Character, the Principle of National Ortholinon Applies to All National States.

There are three kinds of national ortholinon throughout the world.

Firstly, the national sovereignty resides with the household of the ruler: in this case, the house of the ruling sovereign hands down the sovereignty from generartion to generation as a hereditary entity. The Emperor of Japan belongs to this category.

Secondly, the sovereignty is believed to reside with the people as a whole or is held by some political thinkers to reside with the whole nation, but, in its actual form, it resides with the hereditary imperial or royal house as in the case of the British Empire and Italy. There are many other countries in Europe that belong to this category.

Thirdly, the sovereignty resides with the whole nation but is represented by a President who is elected by the collective will of the people: the Presidency is assumed in turns. The U.S.A., Germany, Switzerland, Brazil and many other countries belong to this kind.

Thus, the national ortholinon is represented either by the sovereign of a state such as, for example, an emperor, king or president; or by the family or household of an hereditary sovereign. In supreme morality, therefore, an imperial household, a king's house or the president is respected, being identified with the state. Because the national happiness is attained by the governing activity of the sovereignty, the person who holds the sovereignty, whether he may be an emperor, a king or a president, should be identified as or with the national parent. In supreme morality, therefore, not only the Japanese imperial house but also the rulers of the states other than Japan are each respected as the leading exponent of a rightful national ortholinon."[4]

Because of the change of time, some expressions in this quotation and their interpretation need to be modified.

Firstly, in the case of Japan, she is not the former Empire of Japan and the status of the Emperor has changed from "the Head of the State who has the right to govern"[5] to "the symbol of the State and of the unity of the people, deriving his position from the will of the people with whom resides the sovereign power."[6]

The moral status of the Emperor, however, has not been changed, and as moralogians, we naturally regard the Emperor as the exponent of our national ortholinon.

Secondly, Italy, for one, ceased to be a monarchy from June 2, 1946, and since then has been a republic.

Being well aware of the varieties in national polities, national characteristics and history, Dr. Hiroike admits varieties of form of respect towards a national ortholinon in each country. He maintains, however, that there should be no difference in spirit. He writes as follows:

> "As for most countries in the world which are different from Japan in their national structure, civil polity and racial character, there is much doubt as to the qualification of the subject of the national ortholinon and also concerning the spirit and method of each nation to serve its own respective subject of the national ortholinon. These problems have been utterly ignored to this day among the intellectuals of the world, so here, it seems especially necessary for me to explain them. As mentioned above, all conduct, to be moral, must be fitted to the circumstances, so the method of the conduct may vary, but the spirit of the conduct and the moral principle of practising it should always be the same. This, therefore, is applied to the question concerning the national ortholinon. Though the qualifications of the national ortholinon differ from country to country, the substance of the national ortholinon should be in principle the same in any country. Next, though the form in which the nation respects its own national ortholinon differs according to the difference in the national structure, civil polity and racial character, the principle that the nation must respect its own national

ortholinon should be applied in any coutry. These are because, judging from the sociological point of view, the principle of the formation of a state is the same in any country, and at the same time the principle in the practical method of ruling a nation is also the same"[7]

From these quotations we can understand that

1. Dr. Hiroike had the intention to apply the principle of national ortholinon not only to Japan but also to other countries.
2. He recognized the varieties of the status and nature of national ortholinons in various countries.
3. The main body of national ortholinon may be a single person, such as Emperor, King, or President but sometimes national ortholinon refers to plural persons such as those of an Imperial House, a Royal family, preferably hereditary ones.
4. In the case of a republic, the President of the state is, according to Dr. Hiroike, regarded as the national ortholinon. He is silent about or does not make any reference to the separation of powers into executive, legislative and judicial branches.
5. In the case of monarchy, the monarch or king is regarded as the national ortholinon. Even in Dr. Hiroike's lifetime, monarchy was going downhill. Many kings now exist only in a ceremonial status.

Now let us consider the national ortholinon in the United Kingdom and the United States.

The National Ortholinon in the United Kingdom

Most Japanese moralogians believe that the Queen of

England is the national ortholinon to the English people. Dr. Lauwerys said that "to consider her a national ortholinon would be a mistake...The national ortholinon in England would be a combination of the Crown, the Parliament, the Court, and the Church." As the Crown and the head of the Church are represented in the same person, there are actually three. Historically and realistically speaking, Dr. Lauwerys' view seems to be more acceptable by the English people. Since the time of Magna Carta (1215), the Crown has been checked by the aristocrats and Parliament; the constitutional monarchy and Parliamentalism have developed in England. Toynbee writes as follows:

> "Why did the Transalpine feudal monarchy grow into a constitutional monarchy in England when it gave way to an absolute monarchy in France?
>
> 'It was because the English monarchy became national before it ceased to be feudal, at a time when the French monarchy still remained feudal only. When then the feudal element disappeared, as it ultimately did in both kingdoms, in England its place was taken by a government in which the Estates had already begun to share; in France there was no power in existence to replace the feudal monarchy but the uncontrolled power of an absolute king.' (C. H. McIlwaine in, *The Cambridge Medieval History*, vol. vii (1932, Cambridge Univ. Press), pp. 709–10.)"[8]

The Court and the Church also have played important roles in national life. The national ortholinon in England could be therefore considered as a complex of the four: the Crown, Parliament, the Court and the Church, and the Crown should stand as the central symbol of the English national ortholinon.

The National Ortholinon in the United States

As the United Kingdom is a constitutional monarchy, the status of the English national ortholinon has some similarity with that of the Japanese one; but the United States is a republic and has a President, not a Crown. The hereditary principle of succession which is homogeneous to the ortholinon principle cannot be found in the United States. It reminds me of Henry Adams. His great-grandfather was John Adams, second President of the United States, and his grandfather was John Quincy Adams, the sixth President of the U.S. His father was Charles Francis Adams, minister to England during the Civil War, and one of ablest diplomats America has produced. James Truslow Adams writes in his 'Introduction' to *The Education of Henry Adams* (by Henry Adams) as follows:

> "By the time the line reached Henry, the accumulated weight of great abilities and great offices had become crushing in a democracy. In no other American family, and in few anywhere, have ability and service been so conspicuous generation after generation without a break. In an aristocracy such a family would have been given a title, and have become a continuing entity as a family in the political and social life of the country. In a democracy there could be no such scaffolding built, so to say, about the structure."[9]

Heny Adams himself wrote of his childhood experience filled with deep emotion or a sense of failure, "The Irish gardener once said to the child: 'You'll be thinkin' you'll be President too?"[10] Here let us notice a great difference between the basic philosophy of ortholinon principle and that of American Democracy. Any moralogian who wants to introduce moralogy to the United States cannot evade this problem. At first I will quote Dr. Hiroike's statement:

> "the ortholinon principle does not contain an expression of such a shallow idea as to respect vacuously an individual's great power and virtue which have flowered for the time being and as not to question the degree of his morality or the final result of his enterprise…the principle of respect for the ortholinon regards, from the standpoint of natural law, the whole series of each respective ortholinon as one individual entity."[11)]

This aspect of the ortholinon principle, therefore leads to the hereditary principle of succession, which is incompatible with the individualistic and egalitarian aspect of American Democracy. Max Lerner writes as follows:

> "American was in conception a classless society. Behind its settlement and growth was a heritage partly borrowed from revolutionary Europe, partly shaped by the American experiment. It included four related elements: hatred of privilege, the religion of equality, open channels of opportunity, and rewards based on achievement and not on birth or rank.
> …In the phrase that Jefferson picked up and adapted from an English rebel, "the mass of mankind has not been born with saddles on their backs, nor a favored few booted and spurred, ready to ride them legitimately by the grace of God."[12)]

This basic philosophy of American Democracy comes, of course, from American experience. Alexis de Tocqueville writes, "It may be said that on leaving the mother country the emigrants had, in general, no notion of superiority one over another. The happy and the powerful do not go into exile, and there are no surer gurantees of equality among men than poverty and misfortune."[13] This is the social basis of "Men are created equal" in "The Declation of Independence." The religious basis of this egalitarianism comes from the Christian intuition of man; but there are many differences among men. As James Bryce says, therefore, "To reconcile this Natural Inequality as a Fact with the principles of Natural Equality as a Doctrine is one of the chief problems which every government has to solve."[14]

When we discuss the polity of the United States, we have to study the birth of the Republic.

The American War of Independence began in 1775 with the firing, at Concord, Massachusetts, of "the shot heard round the World."[15] It was not a mere revolt against George III. Bernard Bailyn, Winthrop Professor of History at Harvard says, "Its original aims were quite narrowly political and constitutional: it began as a protest movement against the misuse of power and the violation of constitutional principles by the ministry of George III."[16] The result was, however, a revolution against England (including George III). Dr. Hiroike, in spite of that, showed his respect to George Washington and the American national character,[17] though he did not elaborate on the reason. Dr. Hiroike's attitude reminds me of Confucius who from necessity approved T'ang Wang of the Yin Dynasty and Wu Wang of the Chou Dynasty by saying that their revolutions were essentially helpful for the welfare of the people. History is depicted in neither black nor white, but in various shades of gray.

Now let us consider wherther the President of the United States could be the national ortholinon in a moralogical sense.

If the national ortholinon means a person who has practised

supreme morality, and preferably a direct descendant of the hereditary throne or a successor of the family who have practised supreme morality generation after generation, the President of the United States cannot be the national ortholinon. The national ortholinon in this sense can be applicable only to the Japanese Imperial household, and Dr. Hiroike obtained this concept from the Japanese Imperial House which has enjoyed an unbroken line of succession. Dr. Hiroike, however, wanted to broaden the meaning of the national ortholinon and he regarded the President of the country as a national ortholinon, though it may be a fictionalized form of it.

The President and Presidency in the United States have been studied and discussed by many scholars. James Bryce asks "Why great men are not chosen Presidents"[18] and finds many defects in the Presidency. One of the defects is "that the presidential election, occurring once in four years, throws the country for several months into a state of turmoil, ..."[19] which "produces a discontinuity of policy."[20] The system of the presidential election reminds us of the continuation of prosperity on the sacrifice of regicide which is described vividly by James G. Frazer in his *The Golden Bough*. Frazer writes of the reason of regicide as follows:

> "To guard against these catastrophes it is necessary to put the king to death while he is still in the full bloom of his divine manhood, in order that his sacred life, transmitted unabated force to his successor, may renew its youth..."[21]

The presidential election is, of course, not so violent as is described above. Some critics say that it is performed by votes instead of bullets. It could therefore be said that Democracy contains somewhat violent elements.

Moralogy teaches us to be more sincere and helpful when the national ortholinon happens to be wrong or even vicious. It may sound too good-natured on the side of people. What moralogy teaches us is to have a great benevolence and sincerity based on God's will or spirit of salvation; but is it possible to persuade all Americans to practice such great sincerity and loyalty to the President? No, I don't think it is possible. The next presidental campaign against the new President starts on the very day of the Inauguration. Are they traitors against the President? No; it is permitted in American Democracy. America is a very dynamic and mobile society. You can find freedom, vitality and openness. The American people has chosen dynamism in a democratic society rather than stability and calmness in a hereditary society. As Max Lerner writes, "You cannot have at the same time the freedom and fluidity of an open society and the values of security that go with a closed one."[22]

After all, there could be no presidential family which has practised supreme morality for centuries and enjoyed the Presidency for many generations, though Dr. Hiroike hoped to create such families in the republic.[23]

American government stands on the principle of checks and balances, and the separation of powers. It is because Henry Steele Commager writes, "To the Founding Fathers history taught one clear lesson: that all governments tended towards tyranny: that men in power were always tempted to abuse their power; that no governments or men could be trusted to refrain from the misuse of power."[24] On this ground, Dr. Lauwerys said, "A President is declared by law not to be the national ortholinon." The American national ortholinon would be the complex of the President, the Court, and the Congress. As is the case of the English national ortholinon, I would like to say that the President should be the central symbol of the national ortholinon. Or rather, the Presidency or the American spirit behind a living President would be the national ortholinon. When a President seriously damages the spirit of the national ortholinon, he would be, like Nixon, impeached, though the people must help the President to be virtuous in every possible way.

Anyway, "the center of gravity of American political life" has moved from the other two branches over to the Excutive power; and the system which in the early phase of the Republic was called "Congressional government," and in the *laissez-faire* decades of the late nineteenth century "government by judiciary," must now be called "Presidential government."[25] The status of the President, therefore, is growing more important than before.

IV

From the previous considerations, we have understood that when the Institute of Moralogy tries to internationalize moralogy, it has to disengage the essentials from Japanese accidental accretions. I believe this would be approved by Dr. Hiroike from his fragmentary comments, though the operation of winnowing should be deliberate.

As we have observed in the previous discussion, there are great gaps between East and West. The gap ranges from trivial customs and institutions to even the basic philosophy of life and the world. Can we bridge the gap? I believe we can and must close the gap in the time of the 'annihilation of distance.' Dr. Hiroike tried to offer a common forum for world morality. Democracy seems, at the first look, to be incompatible with the traditional view of moralogy; however, if we look deeper into the essence of Democracy, we can find that Democracy is rooted in the depths of Christianity and Hellenism which moralogy shares in common. Anyone, whether he may be an Easterner or a Westerner, will be moved by St. Paul's passages from 1 Corinthians 13: 1–8 as follows:

> "1. If I speak in the tongues of men and of angels, but have not love, I am a noisy gong or a clanging cymbal.
> 2. And if I have prophetic powers, and understand all mysteries and all knowledge, and if I have all faith, so as to remove mountains, but have not love, I am nothing.
> 3. If I give away all I have, and if I deliver my body to be burned, but have not love, I gain nothing.
> 4. Love is patient and kind; love is not jealous or boastful;
> 5. It is not arrogant or rude. Love does not insist on its own way; it is not irritable or resentful;
> 6. It does not rejoice at wrong, but rejoices in the right.
> 7. Love bears all things, believes all things, hopes all things, endures all things.
> 8. Love never ends; as for prophecy, it will pass away; as for tongues, they will cease; as for knowledge, it will pass away."

The ortholinon principle itself is derived from God's will and so it should not be interpreted merely in an institutional sense.[26] It should be a vital force which quickens institutions with the spirit of love for mankind. If we regard the principle of the national ortholinon as a formless, invisible spirit of national unification in accord with the welfare of Mankind, there would be few who would not accept it. I conclude this paper with a sincere prayer that "here on earth God's work must truly be our own."[27]

Chapter V

The Civilizational Soul

Section 3

Two Japanese Masters of the Civilizational Soul: Hiroike Chikuro and Mori Ōgai

Though one of the suggested themes from the committee of the Dublin conference is "Island Civilizations as Cultural Initiators and Receivers," I have slightly modified this to "Japanese Civilization as a Cultural Initiator and a Receiver." This theme is, however, I find, still too broad in the limited time for presentation, I would therefore like to approach this theme by focusing on two great men of modern Japan—Hiroike Chikuro and Mori Ōgai, expecting that, by so doing, I shall inevitably discuss the problems of Japanese civilization in the process of developing my thesis.

I

Frames of Reference

The theme itself implies that there have been major civilizations and peripheral civilizations in the world, whatever the nomenclature may be, and that there have been enconters, challenges and responses among them. When we discuss this kind of topic, I think that Toynbee's ideas of "Challenge and Response"[1] and "Encounters between civilizations in space and time"[2] are extremely useful.

When the influences of major civilizations on peripheral civilizations are dominant, as were the cases of Hellenization, Islamization, Sinicizaiton, Indianization, and Westernization of today, there are three types of responses from the weaker civilizations, i.e., first, Zealotism, which tries to expel foreign influences; second, Herodianism which tries to receive advanced foreign culture, and third, Evangelism, which transcends the above two egoistic "isms" and tries to create a new culture. All these terms are used by Toynbee who utilizes these types of responses found in Judea of Jesus's time—Zealots who were members of a radical political and religious sect who openly resisted Roman rule in Palestine, and King Herod who accepted advanced Hellenism, and Jesus who worked for salvation—as typical examples.[3]

Peripheral civilization

My second frame of reference is the concept of peripheral civilization. Though Toynbee used the term 'satellite' civilization, I prefer 'peripheral' civilization, as the term is employed by Philip Bagby in his *Culture and History*.[4] This is because 'satellite' implies that it has no radiation in itself, nor creativity, and because 'peripheral' indicates something more objective and neutral, and it suggests only its location—not central.

In comparison to the major civilization, the peripheral civilization is receptive, dependent upon the major civilization, less creative, fragile and short-lived. If a peripheral civilization, continues to be subjected to a strong radiation from a major civilization, it is to be absorbed and assimilated by the major civilization and finally it ceases to exist. (For example, Etruscan civilization started as a peripheral civilization to Greek and Roman civilization; it was later, however, absorbed and assimilated.)

Categorizing Japanese civilization

Japanese civilization has been said to share similar characteristic to other peripheral civilizations—for example, passivity and a mixed or electic character. Some Japanese intellectuals are very diffident towards their own civilization by saying that Japanese culture is a hybrid (Kato Shuichi), mixed (Maruyama Masao), and eclectic (Tsurumi Shunsuke), and that Japan is extremely passive and has learned many things from other countries but has not contributed to other world cultures. This last is what Japan must try to achieve from now; but are the former characteristics—hybrid, mixed, and eclectric—undesiable? Great Britain, the United States of America, and the English language itself are all very mixed and hybrid.

Japan started as a civilization peripheral to Chinese civilization in the seventh century, but by the end of the ninth centry it seemed to become independent from Chinese civilization. Dr. Shin Yamamoto[5] points out five phenomena which indicate Japan's independence from Chinese civilization: 1) Changes of Emperors' names from Chinese forms to Japanese ones, 2) Sugawara Michizane's termination of embassies to the T'ang Dynasty in China in 894, 3) The imported *Ritsu ryo seido* (system of law and administration) transformed itself at the end of the ninth century to the tenth century into *Kanpaku seido* (the system of the chief adviser to the Emperor). 4) Buddhism began to be assimilated to the native religion, Shintō, identifying Dainichi Nyorai with Amaterasu Ōmikami—a dual system for the coexistence of Shintoism and Buddhism. 5) Japanization of various fields of arts, *shinden zukuri, yamatoe, wayo, yoseki dukuri*, calligraphy, etc., 6) Invitation of the kana syllabary, in which parts of Chinese characters are borrowed and used phonetically to represent Japanese syllables. This syllabary can represent all of the Japanese language. China has never had such a syllabary system, and so she has a difficulty in expressing phonetically, say, western languages by Chinese characters. The Phoenician alphabet was supposed to have been created from the borrowing of some twenty phonetic symbols from among some 500 Egyptian hieroglyphics. This is an original Phoenecian development, from which the modern alphabet is derived.

Japan has become a civilization again peripheral to the Western civilization since Commander Perry's four Black Ships arrived in 1853, as all other civilizations in the world have become peripheral civilizations. There are many degrees of peripheralness, however, from basic dependency to greater independency. Japan may be classified, as Bagby says, somewhere between a major civilization and a peripheral one.

My thesis how modern Japan, as desclibed above, has coped with the strong influence of Westernization,[6] and how she has managed to retain a clear sense of her own identity—by taking up the examples of two Japanese, Hiroike Chikuro and Mori Ōgai.

II

Mori Ōgai (1862–1922)

Ōgai ranks with Natsume Sōseki as one of the major literary figures of modern Japan, but was more versatile and less imaginative (though his style is just exquisite!) than Sōseki who was an English teacher and a novelist. Ōgai was once called "Thebes's great gates" by Kinoshita Mokutaro: "Mori Ōgai is like the so-called great metropolis of Thebes with one hundred gates. If you go into the east gate, you have a difficulty in exhausting the west gate. One hundred scholars can see only one or two gates and leave the other ninety-eight or ninety-nine gates untouched." His erudition ranges from the humanities, social sciences to the natural sciences, and from East to West. At the age of forty-six (in 1907) he was promoted to the highest rank for a doctor in the army, that of Surgeon General, and was also made Head of the Bureau of Medical Affairs at the Department of War and occupied those posts from 1907 to 1916. In 1917 Ōgai was appointed Director of the Imperial Museum and Library, a post he was to hold until his death five years later. In his last years he concentrated on the biographies of *Shibue Chūsai, Isawa Ranken* and *Hōjō Katei*, a study of Imperial Postumous Names (*Teishiko*), and an unfinished study of era names (*Gengōko*). In the daytime he worked as an army doctor and wrote at night and on holidays. He slept only three to four hours a night. When he died on July 9, 1922, he left thirty-eight large volumes of his works.

Ōgai transplanted European and American literature into Japan: German, French, English, Russian, Austrian, Swedish, Danish, Hungarian, Belgian, Spanish, Norwegian, Irish, Italian, and American. Sometimes his translations are said to surpass in quality the originals; for example, *Sokkyo Shijin* (*Improvisatoren*) by H. C. Andersen, and "Fuyu no O" ("Erling" by Hans Land). He translated Goethe's *Faust* into Japanese in six months. It has remained the most authoritative translation for over half a century. He was also well-versed in both Japanese and Chinese classics.

Through translations and creative writings, he introduced

many Western concepts and names of institutions into Japanese vocabulary. He is one of the builders of the modern Japanese language. We cannot express modern concepts in science, technology, arts in the Japanese language of Chikamatsu Monzaemon or Matsuo Bashou of the Edo period, however great they might have been.

Ōgai played the role of a Herodian but at the same time from his youth, he had a strong cultural identity. When he was studying at Dresden, Germany in 1886, he happened to listen to the derision towards Japan and Japanese culture expressed by Dr. Edmund Naumann, a German geologist. Naumann said that a Japanese steam-ship whose sailors learned from Westerners how to start its engine but forgot to learn how to stop it had to go round and round in Yokohama Bay until the engine stopped naturally. To be fair with Naumann, I will quote another statement of his: "...the undiluted adoption of European culture might weaken instead of strengthen the Japanese, and bring about the collapse of the race." To that Ōgai replied: "What kind of European culture is it which if adopted, brings with it the danger of destruction? Does true European culture not lie in the recognition of freedom and beauty in the purest sense of those words? Is this recognition capable of bringing about destruction?" Richard John Bowring adds the comment: "It was only somewhat later that he was to realize the partial truth of what Naumann had said. The adoption of an alien culture was to set up stresses and threaten to leave a spiritual vacuum that became one of Ōgai's major preoccupations in later life."[7]

He studied hygiene in Germany from 1884 to 1888. In 1891, at the age of thirty, he was awarded a Medical doctorate. He wrote a German diary called *Doitsu Nikki* in Chinese. Later it was translated into Japanese. Because of his personal experience of 'overseas study' in Germany, because of his reading and translations of many kinds of Western books, magazines, and newspapers, and because of his profound and detailed knowledge of Japanese and Chinese cultures, his mind was in conflict between both the East and the West. Japan was struggling to catch up with the level of the West within half a century, which took the West three centuries to achieve. Japan was, as one of his short stories, "Fushinchu" indicates, "under construction" because of her hasty modernization.

"Hebi" (1911) is the story of a beautiful wife who was shocked into becoming a maniac suffering from hallucinations by finding a big snake in her household Buddhist altar in which her mother-in-law's new memorial tablet was enshrined. Otoyosan, this beautiful wife, was educated in Tokyo under the strong influence of Western egalitarianism. She married a good-natured but weak-willed husband, Chitaru Hozumi, whose family was an old wealthy one. She had no sense of respecting any 'authority,' whether it was God, Buddha, parents, or government. She was not obedient to her husband's mother. She was unwilling to join the happy family circle. "The Hozumi family became a house of silence." Then the mother passed away with a lonely heart.

The narrator in the story is a doctor of science. He put the snake from the altar into his creel. The next morning when he was leaving that house, he advised her husband to invite a psychiatrist from Tokyo.

The waves of Western culture had a strong impact on the traditional, Confucian, Buddhistic, feudalistic Japanese society of the end of the Edo era, of the Meiji, Taisho, Showa, and even the Heisei, eras. Otoyosan is a victim of cultural confusions. She has no love, neither Christian love, Buddhist benevolence, nor Confucian virtue—none whatever. There are thousands of Otoyosans even today.

Ōgai created charming female characters in his later years, for example, Osayosan in his "Yasui fujin" (1914), and Iho in *Shibue Chūsai* (1916). Osayosan is the beautiful wife of a Confucian scholar in the Edo era, and Iho is the beautiful and courageous wife of a medical samurai at the end of the Edo era and the early Meiji era, who studies English in her later years. In both stories, Ōgai does not reveal any sense of the resignation or sad pathos which permeate his other works.

In this short sketch, I regret to find that I have touched on only a few things. With his extensive reading and penetrating thought, Ōgai achieved a cultural synthesis of the East and the West. Whenever I read his works, I must confess that I feel fragrance, refreshment. transparence, precision, and beauty of style.

III

Hiroike Chikuro (1866–1938)

Hiroike was an elementary school teacher, a Japanese historian, a grammarian of Classical Chinese, a compiler of the *Kojiruien* (1,000 volumes in Japanese bindings, 51 volumes in Western bindings, the biggest Encyclopaedia of things Japanese from ancient times to the end of the Edo period), a professor of Japanese Shintoism, a Doctor of Law in the history of Chinese and Korean laws, and finally, the founder of Moralogy (moral science)—a peace-making effort, which failed in its opposition to Japanese militarism in China and in preventing the later Japanese-American war.

"I have 'fortunately' become ill."

In 1912 at the age of forty-six, he was stricken with a serious disease that almost took his life. He wrote in his diary:

Section 3 Two Japanese Masters of the Civilizational Soul:
Hiroike Chikuro and Mori Ōgai

"I do not care for severe coldness nor very hot days, worked hard from five in the morning until one after midnight, did not mind fatigue and illness without resting even one hour...really high-spirited." Peripheral nerve paralysis and its accompanying visceral disorders were the result of his accumulated overwork. Hovering between life and death, he engaged in a deep self-examination of his past life. As he had little formal schooling—and in Japan at that time a man's value was measured by his school background—he felt that his work was not fairly evaluated. He worked extremely hard. He had, however, inner complaints and critical attitudes to others and he became very ill. On the night of December 6, 1912, he was on the brink of death. Then he prayed to God. In his dying consciousness, a visionary rope came down from the ceiling and he caught hold of it. He desparately prayed to God to forgive his sin that his past efforts were after all from his selfish effort for academic fame, asking for one year (later he asked for twenty years) more of life in order to write a book for the salvation of mankind. Dramatically, his doctoral dissertation which had been submitted to the Imperial University of Tokyo three years earlier passed on December 7, 1912, just one day after his most critical day. He realized that *success and happiness are not the same thing.*

Another ordeal came to him in April 1915 when he was expelled from a Shintō sect which he had entered a few years earlier. He tried to revitalize that new religion; his spiritual reform plan was bitterly opposed by some executives among the sect dispatched from the Meiji government. When he was expelled, he was penniless and bookless, because he had donated everything he possessed to the sect.

In his plight, he made self-examination after self-examination; he endeavored to purify his self, and resolved to abandon his study of law, by saying that we are not saved by law, only by true morality. He launched a new study of morality and devoted his entire energies to demonstrate the effectiveness of moral practice. From the age of forty-nine to sixty he devoted himself to founding a new moral science in an uncharted sea of learning, and established moralogy in his *Treatise on Moral Science* (3,500 pages) in 1928. [This book was translated into English as *Towards Supreme Morality*, 4 vols. (Institute of Moralogy, Chiba, Japan, 2002)]

Moralogy was his coined word: Latin 'mores' and the Greek suffix 'logia'—thus moralogy (moral science in English—there are many moral sciences in the West, but Hiroike's moral science is very different from them). In order to prevent Confusion he coined the term moralogy.

Supreme morality is morality as practised by the great sages, who gave firm moral direction to mankind's spiritual life, and thereby brought profound inspiration and exerted immeasurable influence throughout history. Up to the present time there have been various models of supreme morality in the world; but Hiroike chose the following models or paradigm figures and discussed their moral streams: those of Socrates of Greece, Jesus Christ of Judea, Buddha of India, Confucius of China, and Amaterasu Ōmikami, the mythical ancestress of the Japanese Imperial Household. Supreme morality is derived from the principles common to each of these five moral streams.[8] Supreme morality has been closely examined and has stood the test from the standpoint of the history of mankind, from the sociological point of view, from present-day scientific standards and also from his own personal experience in life.[9]

Hiroike traced the origins and development of moral instincts, examined the three kinds of morality, i.e., immorality (amorality), ordinary (conventional) morality, and supreme morality, and the respective results of practices of these three kinds of morality, by integrating materials and data from geology, physical geography, biology, the theory of evolution, genetics, ethnography, physiology, anthropology, ethnology, ethnogeny, jurisprudence, psychology, sociology, criminology, the history of legislation, the history of economy, the history of civilizations (world history), the history of morality, Western philosophy, Christian theology, comparative ethnography, criminal anthropology, criminal sociology, animal psychology, social psychology, folk psychology, Shintoism, Confucianism, Buddhism, ethics, etc.

Together with his accumulated knowledge of the Chinese sages and Japanese Shintoism, and Chinese and Japanese history, both of which are rich sources of moral causality, and the historical records of legitimate lines of succession, he created a new moral science which is an integration of, in a sense, Toynbee's higher religions or Jaspers' great philosophers in the *Achsenzeit* and modern sciences.

In his view, supreme morality (including genuine and unbiased faith) is the most powerful energy to create security, peace and happiness for individuals, families, places of work, communities, nations, and the world at large.

Hiroike's advocacy of moralogy and supreme morality is, in Toynbee's term, an evangelical response to the Western impact on Japan.

His aspiration to a missionary spirit to the West was expressed in his letter to Motoyama Hikoichi, President of Osaka Mainichi Newspaper Company in February, 1931 as follows:

> The only purpose of the Orientals' travel about Europe and America has hitherto been to learn something about splendid civilizations or cultures in the West. The purpose

of my travels about Europe and America this time is, however, completely, different from the above mentioned one. That is, my purpose is to elucidate the academic and moral principles consistent in the thoughts and deeds of the world sages whose major sources are lacking in Europe and America, and to show the fundamental method for real evolution of mankind to the wise and common people there and to subject it to their consideration. And after making adequate preparations, I will leave Japan in the summer of this year (1931), at first, for the United States of America, then Great Britain, then the Eurpean Continent, and try to infuse the new thought and new morals into academic circles and practical societies.[10]

We must appreciate his grand spirit; however, the year 1931 was an *Annus Terribilis*, a terrible year, as Toynbee wrote on the first page of *Survey of International Affairs, 1931*: "In 1931, men and women all over the world were seriously contemplating and frankly discussing the possibility that the Western system of Society might break down and cease to work." Many bad things—the Hoover moratorium, Britain's suspension of the gold standard, Japan's military action in Manchuria, etc.—occurred. In May, 1931, the twentieth year after his great illness and the final year of his asking God to extend his life, Hiroike's health deteriorated most seriously again. He gave up his travel plan.

Japan is often criticized, as I wrote in the beginning of this section, as passive and failing to contribute anything cultural to the world; you may, however, find an ardent passion to contribute to world peace and welfare in Hiroike's character and deeds. In his last years until 1938, he worked for peace-making efforts in China and for the prevention of the later Japanese-American war, by writing letters to, and inviting to his Institute of Moralogy, prime ministers Wakatsuki and Saito, and the Grand

Section 3 Two Japanese Masters of the Civilizational Soul: Hiroike Chikuro and Mori Ōgai

Chamberlain Suzuki and several more high ranking officials—which was regarded as a dangerous thing for a private man to do in the then militaristic atmosphere.

In conclusion, Mori Ōgai played the role of a Herodian, but because of his erudition of the East and the West he transcended national boundaries, and obtained universality in his works. Hiroike tried to play the role of an Evangelist by means of moralogy, which is the integration of supreme morality of the world sages and modern sciences. Both were born in an island civilization or a peripheral civilization, and because of that, they were exempt from narrow-minded national arrogance, and received fine cultural fruits from other world civilizations, and responded to the Western impact creatively.

In comparative civilizations, there may be two realms of study: one is a purely descriptive, analytical study of civilizations; the second is an applied study of civilizations—how to advance the welfare and happiness of mankind's civilizations.

Both are important. In the case of Hiroike, however, he classified morality into three types: immorality, conventional morality, and supreme morality. He recommended that mankind in future should practise this supreme morality. He combined both theory and practice. He established the Institute of Moralogy in 1935, and it developed into school education (one university, two senior high schools, one junior high school, and a kindergarden) and social education for 6,000 registered members and 7,000 corporate members and three million listeners and readers under the president Mototaka Hiroike, his great grandson.

Finally, I would like to make a proposal that "supreme morality" could be one of the concepts of post-civilizational society, and that many scholars should pay attention to the study of civilizations from the viewpoint of morality.[11]

Chapter V

The Civilizational Soul

Section 4

The Unprecedentedness of Moralogy Viewed from the History of Western Moral Science

I. Foreword

The main section of this chapter is to elucidate the significance of Chikuro Hiroike's Moralogy, which is also one of various moral sciences in the world. In fact, Hiroike's *magnum opus* is entitled *The Treatise on Moral Science: A First Attempt at Establishing Morlogy as a New Science* (1928). What does "Moralogy as a New Science" mean? I put it in the historical context of Western moral sciences, and try to find out how it differs from other moral sciences, its methodology, contents, and the "unprecedentedness" of its substance. By doing so, I would like to explain why Hiroike coined a new word, Moralogy.

The first example of the term "moral science" in the *OED* is "1828: G. Payne, *Elements of Mental and Moral Science*." But I have found an earlier usage of the term in a letter from Benjamin Franklin to Joseph Priestley on February 8, 1780: "O that moral science were in as fair a way of improvement, that men would cease to be wolves to each other, and that human beings would at length learn what they call improperly humanity!" (*The American Tradition in Literature*, 1990, p. 208). In the same year, 1780, as I mentioned earlier, G. Payne, *Elements of Mental and Moral Science* appeared and also Jeremy Bentham published a book of a utilitarian study of morality, *An Introduction to the Principles of Morals and Legislation*, in which Bentham used "moral science."

II. The Western Moral Sciences

1. Moral Philosophy and Moral Sciences

An early example that moral philosophy implies moral 'sciences' is Thomas Hobbes's *Leviathan* 1651. The *OED* writes "Moral science has in recent times been used in the same senses as 'moral philosophy.' In the 17th and 18th centuries, the concept of science was used as 'philosophy'. Therefore moral philosophy can be understood as moral science.

2. James Beattie's *Elements of Moral Science*

As far as I know, the first occasion on which "moral science" was used in the title of a book was in James Beattie's *Elements of Moral Science* (Press of Mathew Crey, Philadelphia, 2 vols., 1790–1793). Beattie was born on October 25, 1735 in Kincardineshire, Scotland. In 1760, at the tender year of 25, Beattie was installed as Professor of Moral Philosophy and Logic at his alma mater Marischal College. He published *An Essay on the Nature and Immutability of Truth in Opposition to Sophistry and Skepticism* (hereinafter "Essay on Truth"). As the title implies, Beattie was one of the Scottish 'Common Sense' philosophers who reacted against David Hume's metaphysical skepticism which asserts common sense is illusionary and so unreliable. But Beattie supported the basic soundness of common sense, on which his moral science was built. Dugald Stewart (1753–1828) took a similar line.

The honors piled up thick and fat, and the *Essay* was soon translated into French, German, and Dutch and his fame spread to the New World as well.

His final book was *Elements of Moral Science* (1st vol., 1790, 2nd vol., 1793) which deal with a wide range of topics such as psychology, the faculty of speech, language, sensation, consciousness, memory, sympathy, and so on. Beattie writes, "The mind of man may be improved, in respect, first of action, and secondly, of knowledge. The practical part, therefore, of this Abstract philosophy consists of two parts, Moral Philosophy (strictly so called), which treats of the improvements of active or moral powers; and Logic, which treats of the improvement of our intellectual faculties. Thus we see that the moral sciences may be reduced to four, Psychology, Natural Theology, Moral Philosophy, and Logic" (vol. 1, pp. iv-xxv). Vol. I has 438 pages, vol. II has 688 pages, total pages has 1,126 pages, though voluminous he wrote beautifully and readable enough to read through. We may find a well-read and well-balanced scholar of the end of the 18th century Scotland. But behind these quotations from many books the author's faith in Christianity could be strongly felt and also his conviction is expressed in poetical language. (He was renowned as a poet.) The immortality of the soul and religious and moral causality are strongly demonstrated. (vol. I, pp. 414–438) I am sorry not to describe more in detail here, Beattie clearly stated in an age of slavery in the United States that racial segregation was not acceptable. But Beattie was not gone enough to demand Abolitionism in an age of slavery, and it was unfortunately premature, when we consider the case of Francis Wayland's repeated revisions of his *Moral Science* (since the first edition of

1835) toward slavery according to the progress of time. Beattie's *Moral Science* (which is moral philosophy in content) is an outstanding book in his time.

3. Francis Wayland's *The Elements of Moral Science*

The first work to be noted here is Francis Wayland's *The Elements of Moral Science* (1st ed., 1835). Wayland (1796–1865) was renowned as the President of Brown University (1827–1855), and before that he was pastor of the First Baptist Church of Boston (1821–1826). His fame even reached Japan, where *The Elements*, introduced to the country by Yukichi Fukuzawa, became popular. In it, Wayland writes (p. 1), "Ethics, or Moral Philosophy, is the Science of Moral Law." As to moral causality, he notes (p. 4), "In *morals*, the result is frequently long delayed; and the time of its occurrence is always uncertain." Strangely enough, or perhaps I should rather say, understandably, enough, Hiroike did not mention Wayland in his *Treatise*, because Wayland's *Elements of Moral Science* does not try to study the causal relationship between moral practice and the agent's happiness. Instead, it elucidates topics such as "moral law," "moral action," "conscience," "intention," "the nature of virtue," "self-love," "prayer," "the observance of the Sabbath," etc. He sustained his argument mainly by his own reasoning, but supported it with quotations from the Old and New Testaments, Shakespeare, Bishop Butler and Isaac Newton. An edition of Wayland's *Elements of Moral Science*, with a detailed introduction by Joseph L. Blau, was published by Harvard University Press in 1963.

Ethical Topics Analyzed in Wayland's *Moral Science*
Moral law
Moral action

The moral quality of actions
Conscience or the moral sense
The manner in which decision of conscience is expressed
Rules for moral conduct
The nature of virtue
Human happiness
Self-love
Natural religion
Relation between natural and revealed religion
The Holy Scriptures (The Old Testament and the New Testament)
Love of God, or Piety
The cultivation of a devotional spirit
Prayer
The observance of the Sabbath
Duties to men
Justice and veracity
The duty of slaves (p. 207).   This part was revised in later editions.
The right of property
Oaths
The general duty of chastity—the law of marriage, the rights and duties of parents and children
Moral education (p. 310)
Duties of man as a member of civil society
Duties of citizens
The law of benevolence (p. 360)

4. Leslie Stephen's *The Science of Ethics*

Half a century after Wayland, though, Leslie Stephen published *The Science of Ethics* (1882), an attempt to combine ethics with Darwin's theory of evolution.   "[A]fter Spencer's

Data, this is the first book which worked out an ethical view determined by the theory of evolution." (Internet Encyclopedia of Philosophy). In it, Stephen writes (p. 11), "The accepted test of true scientific knowledge is a power of prediction." He analyzed and reasoned about many topics connected with morality, including "utility," "individualism and society," "race and social organization," "the virtue of temperance and the virtue of truth," "knowledge, conscience, shame, happiness as a criterion, utilitarianism, expediency, morality and happiness, moral discipline, self-sacrifice," etc., as minutely as his predecessors had done, and was obviously trying to elucidate moral causality. But as Hiroike sympathetically explained (see Section II, "Difficulties of Moral Science", pp. 9–21), Stephens failed in his enterprise because of the "imperfection of science generally, hopeless complexity of the problem of individual conduct, absence of a scientific psychology and so on." Stephen himself concludes that "there is no absolute coincidence between virtue and happiness" (p. 434), and he writes, "the science of ethics deals with realities" (p. 450).

Leslie Stephen is famous as the first editor of the *Dictionary of National Biography* (1886–91). He published the first 20 volumes among 26, and he retired from the editor-in-chief because of overwork in 1891. His main works are:

The History of English Thought in the Eighteenth Century, 1876

The Science of Ethics, 1882

The English Utilitarians, 1900

English Literature and Society in the Eighteenth Century, 1904

and his daughter is Virginia Woolf (1882–1941), an elegant author, feminist, essayist, publisher.

Leslie Stephen was an orthodox Utilitarian. After Spencer's

Data (1879), *The Science of Ethics* (1882) is the first book which worked out an ethical view determined by the theory of evolution. He followed Mill and Darwin as an ally of the empirical and utilitarian creed;

> The phrase "moral science" seems to have been well-known in the 19th century; for example, Ralph Waldo Emerson (1803–1882), the Sage of Concord, used it in *The Conduct of Life*, The chapter VI (*The Complete Works*, vol. VI, pp. 240–241).

Another great scholar to be noted here is Henry Sidgwick (1838–1900), who was one of the most influential ethical philosophers of the Victorian era, and his work continues to exert a powerful influence on Anglo-American ethical and political theory. His masterpiece is *The Methods of Ethics* (1st ed., 1874; 7th ed., 1901). Sidgwick describes how each method may provide its own definition of the ultimate goal of ethical conduct. *The Methods of Ethics* defines three basic methods of ethics: 1) egoistic hedonism, 2) intuitionism, and 3) universalistic hedonism. The analysis of these methods attempts to determine the extent to which they are compatible or incompatible. Sidgwick describes how each method may provide its own definition of the ultimate goal of ethical conduct. For egoistic hedonism, the private happiness of each individual may be the ultimate good. For intuitionism, moral virtue or perfection may be the ultimate good. For universalistic hedonism, the general happiness of all individuals may be the ultimate good. Sidgwick describes how each of these methods may define rational principles of conduct and how they may each interpret moral duty differently.

Noah Porter (1811–1892) was the President of Yale

University and, according to Herbert W. Schneider, "in many ways the greatest and most erudite of the professors of philosophy" (*A History of American Philosophy*, Forum Books New York, 1946, 1957, p. 163). Even so, in *The Elements of Moral Science: Theoretical and Practical* (New York, C. Scribner and Sons, 1885), Porter could only go so far as to say (p. 7) that, "moral science is the science of duty, and to study duty scientifically both psychologically and philosophically." In his analysis of moral science, "science" remained on the level of analyses of ethical terms such as duty, obligation, perception or volition. This, of course, was not his fault, but was rather the inevitable result of the way the times lagged. Not only was there the "imperfection of science", as we saw in the case of Leslie Stephen, but there was also the underdevelopment of societies in general and of the corresponding social science, which give us the impression that the moral science of the time was rather old-fashioned. The "science" in moral science was at best partially the theory of evolution.

The emancipation of the slaves was finally realized in the U.S.A. in 1865. Wayland's moral science was revised in various later editions.

The 20th Century

After the First World War (1914–1918), Oswald Spengler published *Der Untergang des Abendlandes* (1919–22) and T. S. Eliot wrote "The Waste Land" in 1922. People in the West were shocked to see their homeland, the center of their civilization, become a battlefield between the Central Powers (Germany, Austria-Hungary and Turkey) and the Allied Powers (mainly France, Britain, Russia, Italy and Japan). People awoke to the urgent need for world peace after the First World War, which meant that the situation for moral science was completely different to what it had been before the early 20th century. It was at this moment that Hiroike's Moralogy appeared.

III. The Advent of Hiroike's Moralogy: Distinct from all previous ethics or moral philosophy

Moralogy as a science to study the effects of the practice of morality (*mos* or *mores* (*moralis*) + logy = moralogy, which was newly coined word by Hiroike)

The process in the making of moralogy
1. His interests in religions and thoughts: Engagements in the woks of the Ise Shrines. Hiroike is responsible for the compilations of more than half of fifty-one volumes of the *Kojiruien*, his publications: *The Shrines of Ise*, 1908. He became interested in Tenrikyo, a sect of Shintoism, *The Chinese Grammar, An Introduction to Far Eastern Law, An Outline of Chinese Law*. He was awarded the Degree of LL.D, by *A Study of Ancient Kinship Law in China*, on December 10th, 1012. He began to launch a study of moralogy (*Treatise*, Chap. I, p. 26).
2. His health problem. Overwork, 1904, nervous breakdown in 1909. Shattered by nervous collapse leads to radical conversion. Its contents are subtly hinted that he criticized himself that his former efforts are after all self-interested and so his effort from now should be entirely for the benefit of others and world peace. But we may find more in detail of his inner life.
3. Social problems. Labor problem in the beginning of the 20th century. Social problems such as socialism, syndicalism, etc. And wars such as the First World War, etc.
4. Great accumulated distresses (criticized by Tenrikyo, and consequently dismissed from it. His devotion changed from a

single religion to the building a comprehensive learning called moralogy. Here I would like to make a special attention to the Ise Jingū, the Ancestral Shrine of the Japanese Emperors and the Fundamental Characters of Japan (1915). Because Hiroike explicitly explain his conversion, it seems to be easy to understand. Yes, it is easy to understand, if we could decipher his erudite Japanese. We are confronted with many quotations from *Kojiki, Nihonshoki*, and other Japanese classics, old folkways and traditions, Confucian classics such as *the Great Learning* (Ta hsueh), the Doctrine of the Mean (Chung yun), the *Confucian Analects*, the *Mencius* (*Meng-tzu*). The Book of Changes, (the Yi-king, the *Scripture of Documents, the Book of Songs or the Book of Poetry, the Record of Ritual, the Spring and Autumn Annals*

John K. Fairbank, Edwin O. Reishaur, Albert M. Craig, *East Asia, Tradition and Transformation*, Herbert University, 1973, Houghton Mifflin.

An unpunctuated Chinese composition

The Contents of *Treatise on Moral Science*
Chap. I Introduction
Chaps. II-XI From Man's position in the universe to the development of man: makings of body and mind and soul and conventional morality in history
Chaps. XII-XIII Supreme Morality of the four sages and Amaterasu
Chap. XIV Contents of Supreme Morality
Chap. XV Observations on the effects of the practice of Supreme morality, conventional morality
    Chapter 11 of Hiroike's *Treatise* is entitled, "On the

Development of Civilization as a tendency and on the Qualitative Development of Morality" (T. II, 109–144). Ordinary, conventional morality is imperfect, and the supreme morality, which was practiced by the ancient sages of the East and West "may be likened to the polar star that shines brightly alone in its own sector of space" (T. II, 111). Before embarking on the study of the sages, Hiroike cautiously praises cosmopolitanism and humanism, commending Hugo Grotius' *De Jure Belli ac Pacis*, 1625, Immanuel Kant's *Zum ewigen Frieden*, Woodrow Wilson and the League of Nations, and others.

Hiroike tackled this problem squarely in his *Treatise on Moral Science* (1928). He tried to identify the causal link between moral practice and the destinies of its practitioners by investigating not individual cases (with the exception of outstanding ones), but the cases of groups (T, III, 383). A prerequisite for this study is to define the qualities of morality: immorality, conventional morality, and supreme morality, and the various results of the practice of each type. Such a causal study is not simple. Mere external and internal interpretations are not enough. Unless we include the moral and religious interpretations of external events, we cannot discover the deep significance of life. Dr. Hiroike confessed, "I *happily* suffered from a serious illness." Under normal conditions, the word *happily* could not be part of this sentence. But in its true meaning, his serious illness turned out to be a blessing and part of his enlightenment and salvation. He introduced the principle of perfecting one's moral character into the realm of moral causality. Only by doing this can we solve difficult problems that are centuries old.

1. The application of modern sciences (from the end of the 19th century to the 1920s) to the system of Moralogy

Hiroike writes [quotation, T. I, 84]: One example of the application of the theory of evolution to the Buddhist doctrine of *dasa dharma-dhatu* (the ten realms of living beings) is as follows: aruras, tiryancs, pretas, narakas, devas, sravaka (the original meaning here is a person who had the chance of hearing Buddha's voice), pratyakabuddha (a person who tries to get enlightenment without his master, and does not try to save other people), bodhisattva (a Buddha elect, but one who has vowed to remain in the world to work for the enlightenment and salvation of others), tathagata (a person who has attained Buddhahood). If Hiroike had known of Karl Jung, he might have included a psychological interpretation of human nature.

2. Hiroike's Methods

a) Historical study: the development of human beings from time immemorial, from ancient times through to medieval and modern times.

b) The development of an individual from infancy through childhood and youth to old age, including physiological, mental and social aspects.

[remainder of this section is unchanged]

c) Unique viewpoints of ordinary, conventional morality and supreme morality. The teachings of the world sages.

Hitherto, ethicists had analyzed the theory of ethics minutely in their moral sciences, but they had never categorized morality as Hiroike did in Chapters 8 to 11. There is too much to mention in detail here but it is all very interesting.

d) The lengthy generational sources for moral causality. See Shi Ji vol xxxvi and "The Descendants of the Ancient Sages" (T. II, 331–337).

Chapter XIII The Sacred virtue of Amaterasu Ōmikami Who Laid the Foundations of Japan's Imperial House, and the Real Cause of the Unbroken Line of Succession of That House.

Hiroike summarizes the most important moral maxim from Amaterasu Ōmikami's Concealment in the Heavenly Rocky Cave as "Benevolence, Tolerance, and Self-Examination." Hiroike writes, "According to classical scholars who have answered my [Hiroike's] questions, who follows in the *Kojiki* version seems to mean ultimately that the features of Amaterasu Ōmikami were reflected in the mirror which though she was born so beautiful according to the *Nihonshoki*, her 'bright splendor penetrated all six sides', after she had practiced self-discipline in the secluded life of the Heavenly Cave, she showed the noblest of features beyond comparison. Uzume no Mikoto then explained and Futotama no Mikoto and Ame no Koyane no Mikoto immediately presented the mirror for her inspection. Thereupon Amaterasu Ōmikami accepted the nation-wide apology and came out of the Heavenly Cave so that the sun was again illuminating the universe. This is why she has the honorific title of Amaterasu Ōmikami (the Great Deity that lightens all Heaven).

That Amaterasu Ōmikami's features underwent change as a result of her seclusion in the Heavenly Cave was reported by the ancient people. The existence of such a legend of the ancient times when the sciences were not as well as developed as they are now may probably be a proof that it existed as a fact (T. II, 452–3). This part reminds me of the Transfiguration of Jesus Christ (Matt. 17: 1–13, and Mark 9: 1–13) and the transfiguration of a Japanese Buddhist saint and founder of the Shingon School Kūkai (774–835) at Seiryouden Palace (Genkoushakusho 『元亨釈書』).

Chapter XIV   The Principle, Substance and Content of Supreme Morality

This chapter is the central one of this great book, and its content is rich and profound. It is impossible to elaborate on it here given the constraints of time. I can only sketch a brief outline.

Justice and Benevolence
The Theory of the Precedence of Duty over Right
Self-renunciation
Principle of Absolute God
Ortholinon Principle, 111-
Enlightenment and Salvation
Pure Orthodox Learning

The key items above are interrelated to one another and each of them is indwelling in a circular fashion, as follows:

Hiroike writes: "From ages past the sages and men of great intelligence in the world generally considered the substance of God or Realty to be justice and benevolence" (T. III, 23). "In Chinese philosophy" (Book of *the Golden Mean*, chap. 20), "Sincerity is the law of Heaven. And sincerity is in accord with natural law, and natural law is the expression of the mind of God" (T. III, 24). "In the West, interpretations of the natural law by philosophers, ethicists and jurists are diversified, but they have the following basic understanding in common: the natural law is the law of God and the essence of the law is justice, that is, the mean, average, equality and the like" (T. III, 25).

Human nature has both goodness and sinfulness. In supreme morality, we are required to sacrifice ourselves for the atonement of those sins we have consciously or unconsciously committed towards God and towards men on the one hand, and for the future perfection of our characters on the other hand (T. III, 55). Here is no self-righteousness concerning one's seemingly moral conduct.

One Primal Universal God is Reality, which is "the ultimate source of all cosmic phenomena." "Absolute, being transcendent over time and space." Actually alive in the universe, a living existence at work ever since the beginning of time without beginning, as a working 'personality' governing all things." In Japanese tradition the deity to be identified with Reality is known as Ame no Minakanushi no Kami; in Chinese tradition, Tian, Tian Di, or Shang Di. In Buddhism, which at first had no positive interest in the idea of a personal deity, Dharma or Dharmakaya corresponds in meaning. So does Jehovah or God in Christianity. It must be noted that all these names are suggestive of certain religious or racial associations and likely to be detrimental to the universal nature of God. In naming the object of its faith, supreme morality adopts none of these parochial names" (T. III, 97). "The second concept of kami, in religious interpretations, is that of the incarnate God, alleged to be Reality appearing a human form in actual human society" (T. III, 97). This concept "has certain difficulty in meeting the general rational thinking of the day. ...In so far as history and reason can testify the only possible interpretation after all is this: that the supreme moral practice of the incarnate God caused him to be identified with the primal universal God. A few illustrations are Amaterasu Ōmikami, Śākyamuni, and Jesus Christ" (T. III, 98).

The Analects of Confucius, referring to the character of Confucius, say that he was completely free from the four ills— arbitrariness, obstinacy, prejudice and selfishness. In Christianity, repentance means turning from egoism to godliness. In Buddhism, the boddhisattva is said to be entirely selfless, having both spirit and body immersed in the wisdom of Buddha. This selflessness, or renunciation of self, is really an important moral creed if man is to enjoy happiness, this one condition being the standard to distinguish a sage from an ordinary person because all so-called sages are selfless (T. III, 82–83).

As to the enlightenment and salvation, "The teachings and deeds of Socrates, Christ, Śākyamuni and Confucius do not always appear to be the same. They are in fact the same, however, in that all four sages devoted themselves to the enlightenment and salvation of the human spirit according to the great universal law of nature" (T. II, 390).

Hiroike then moved on to elucidate supreme morality in order to build a new civilization. In this sense he is very progressive. He quickened the letter of Moralogy with the spirit of his sublimely enthusiastic aspiration.

IV. What should be done for the future of Moralogy

Today, in 2009, the general tendency in thought is a democratic and individualistic current of thought, though this trend is sometimes criticized. In this context, Moralogical thought can seem to be conservative, and indeed it is so. We are in too much haste to think in terms of a time span of many generations and centuries. American thought is, generally speaking, democratic and individualistic. In his *Democracy in America* (ed. H. Reeve, revised Francis Bowen, 2 vols., Vintage Books, New York, 1945), Alexis de Tocqueville used the word "individualism" to denote the American national character for the first time (II, II, ii., trans. H. Reeve, 1840). Mark Twain wrote *The Adventures of Huckleberry Finn* (1844) in which the Duke and King are rapscallions and royalty itself is merely an accepted imposture on the raft on the Mississippi. They are uprooted people (Oscar Handlin, *The Uprooted*, New York, 1951). Aristocratic ranking has no worth on the American frontier.

American society is outwardly a society of equality: Man is created equal. In reality, however, there are big discrepancies between and among social and financial classes. Recently, some business leaders have shamelessly taken huge bonuses in spite of the bankruptcy of their own companies. See Benjamin Barber, *An Aristocracy of Everyone: The Politics of Education and the Future of America* (New York, Ballantine Books, 1992). Hiroike praised American Independence and the country's national character, as well as such founding fathers as George Washington, John Adams, Thomas Jefferson and Benjamin Franklin (T. III, 147 and elsewhere).

Henry Adams has written fascinating books about medieval Europe and modern times: *Mont-Saint-Michel and Chartres: A Study of the Thirteenth-Century Unity,* and *The Education of Henry Adams: A Study of Twentieth-Century Multiplicity.* The 13th century had an integral symbol of faith in the Virgin, and the 20th century had the dynamo. However we cannot go back to the 13th century Europe, when man had the highest idea of himself as a unit in a unified universe, however good this might have been. We have many problems, such as global warming, the environment, disturbances to the global ecosystem, the manipulation of life by medical and nuclear technology, and so forth. In this cosmic 21st century, there is an urgent need for us to have the wisdom and courage to follow the path of supreme morality.

Notes

Chapter I The Vistas of the Comparative Study of Civilizations
*   Presented at the 28th Annual Meeting of the International Society for the Comparative Study of Civilizations at St. Louis, MO. U.S.A. on May 22, 1999.
1) Herman Melville, *Redburn, White-Jacket, Moby-Dick* (New York: The Library of America, 1983), p. 185.
2) Stephen K. Sanderson, ed., *Civilizations and World Systems: Studying World-Historical Change* (Walnut Creek: AltaMira Press, 1995).
3) The *Journal for the Comparative Study of Civilizations,* No. 4 (Reitaku University, 1999), pp. 7–20.
4) See "Comparative Civilization Analysis, As Seen from the West," in the *Journal for the Comparative Study of Civilizations,* No. 4, pp. 13–18, and also "Hermeneutics, Dialogics, and Civilizational Analysis," in *Comparative Civilization*, Vol. 10 (Tokyo: Tosui Shobo, 1994), pp. 209–222.
5) David Wilkinson, "Structural Sequences in the Far Eastern World System/Civilization," in the *Journal for the Comparative Study of Civilizations,* No. 4, pp. 21–62.
6) William H. McNeill, *The Rise of the West: A History of the Human Community, with a Retrospective Essay* (The University of Chicago Press, 1991), xv–xxx. ("The Rise of the

West After Twenty-Five Years," in Sanderson, Stephen K. ed., *Civilizations and World Systems: Studying World-Historical Change* (Walnut Creek: AltaMira Press, 1995), pp. 303–320).

7) Andre Gunder Frank, "The Modern World System Revisited: Rereading Braudel and Wallerstein," in Sanderson, Stephen K. ed., *Civilizations and World Systems: Studying World-Historical Change* (Walnut Creek: AltaMira Press, 1995), pp. 163–194.

8) William Eckhardt, "A Dialectical Evolutionary Theory of Civilizations, Empires, and Wars," in Sanderson, p. 78.

9) Yan Wenming, "Another Ancient Civilization Elucidated by Chinese Archeologists," in *Rekishi Kaidou*, July 1998, pp. 126–131.(厳文明「中国考古学界が解明したもう一つの古代文明」『歴史街道』1998年7月, pp. 126–131).

―――, "Contributions to the Origin of Rice Agriculture in China," in *YRCP (The Yangtze River Civilization Program), Newsletter of the Grant-in-aid Program for COE Research Foundation of the Ministry of Education, Science, Sports and Culture in Japan,* March 1998, Vol. 1, No. 1, pp. 6–8.

10) Takashi Tsutsumi, "What is the oldest Earthenware in the Japanese Archipelago?" in *Rekishi Kaidou*, July 1998, pp. 135. (堤隆「日本列島最古の土器とは？」『歴史街道』1998年7月, p. 135).

See also ―――, "The Oldest Pottery in Japan Archipelago," in *Newsletter of the Grant-in-aid Program for COE Research Foundation of the Ministry of Education, Science, Sports and Culture in Japan,* March 1999, Vol. 2, No. 1, pp. 4–5.

11) Yoshinori Yasuda, "The East Rice Crescent and the West Wheat Crescent," *Journal for the Comparative Study of Civilizations*, No. 4, pp. 15–48. Center for the Comparative Study of Civilizations, Reitaku University, 1999.

See also ―――, "Environment & Civilization," (p. 2) and "The Yangtze River Civilization Program" (pp. 3–4) in *Newsletter of the Grant-in-aid Program for COE Research Foundation of the Ministry of Education, Science, Sports and Culture in Japan,* March 1998, Vol. 1, No. 1, pp. 2–4.

———, "Recent Archaeological Discoveries in the Middle Yangtze Basin, China" in *YRCP (The Yangtze River Civilization Program), Newsletter of the Grant-in-aid Program for COE Research Foundation of the Ministry of Education, Science, Sports and Culture in Japan*, March 1999, Vol. 2, No. 1, pp. 1–4.

12–a) *Saicho and Kūkai* in *Japanese Great Books 5*, Chūōkōronsha, 1977 (『日本の名著 3　最澄　空海』中央公論社, 1977).

12–b) *Selected Works of Hajime Nakamura*, definitive edition, separate volume 5, *Cultural Exchange of the East and the West*, Shunjusha (『中村元選集決定版　別巻 5　東西文化の交流』春秋社), 1998, pp. 194–201.

13–a) *Library of Japanese Thought 5, Kūkai*, Iwanami Shoten (『日本思想大系 5　空海』岩波書店), 1975.

13–b) Ryōtarō Shiba, *Kūkai's Scenery*, 2 vols. Chūōkōronsha, Tokyo (司馬遼太郎『空海の風景』上下, 中央公論社), 1975.

14) *A Series of Esoteric Buddhism 3 Kūkai's Life and Thought*, Shunjusha (『講座密教 3　空海の人生と思想』春秋社), 1976, 1981, p. 245.

15) *The Works of Saint Jiun*, 18 vols. and 1 supplement (『慈雲尊者全集』18 巻 + 補遺　高貴寺), 1921–35.

16–a) *Selected Works of Hajime Nakamura*, definitive edition, separate volume 5, *Cultural Exchange of the East and the West*, Shunjusha (『中村元選集決定版　別巻 5　東西文化の交流』春秋社), 1998, pp. 155–166.

16–b) *The Works of Saint Jiun*, supplement (『慈雲尊者全集』補遺　高貴寺), 1926, 付録 pp. 11–23 及び pp. 33–43.

17) *Library of Japanese Classical Literature 83, Collections of Vernacular Sermons*, Iwanami Shoten (『日本古典文学大系 83　仮名法語集』岩波書店), 1964, pp. 373–396.

18) J. B. Ford, M. P. Richard, P. C. Talbutt eds., *Sorokin & Civilization: A Centennial Assessment with a preface by Roger W. Wescott* (New Brunswick: Transaction Publishers, 1996), p. 56.

19) Barry V. Johnson, *Pitirim A. Sorokin: an Intellectual Biography* (University Press of Kansas, 1995), p. 145. "It

combines the empirical truths of the senses; the rational truths of reason; and the superrational truths of faith." (From Pitirim A. Sorokin, *Social and Cultural Dynamics*, Vol. 4, New York: Bedminster Press, 1941, p. 763).
20) "Integralism, Moralogy, and the New Social Science," in *Journal for the Comparative Study of Civilizations*, No. 4. Center for the Comparative Study of Civilizations, Reitaku University, 1999, p. 73.
21) *Ibid.*
22) Arnold Toynbee, *A Study of History* (Oxford University Press, 1954), Vol. 10, p. 1.
23) *Ibid.*, p. 2.
24) Samuel P. Huntington, *The Clash of Civilizations and the Remaking of World Order* (New York: Simon & Shuster, 1996), p. 318.
25) *Ibid.*, p. 320.

Chapter II Civilization and Religion
Section 1 Civilization and Religion in Toynbee
*   May 8, 1997 at the 26th annual meeting of International Society for the Comparative Study of Civilizations held at Brigham Young University, Provo, Utah.
1) Roman capital numeral and Arabic one in the parenthesis in my text refer to volume and page numbers of Arnold J. Toynbee's *A Study of History*, 12 vols respectively.
2) Illust. and Arabic numerals in my text refer to Toynbee's *A Study of History, Illustrated* (1972) and page numbers.
3) In his later *A Study of History, Illustrated*, 1972, Chap. 40 "Societies of a distinctive species" is used instead of "a higher species of society."
4) English translation of *De Civitate Dei* in Toynbee's *Study* is different from that of Saint Augustine *The City of God*, 2 vols. John Healey's translation, edited by R. V. G. Tasker, introduction by Sir Ernest Baker (Dent, London, Everyman's Library, 1945, 1972).   Toynbee had no need to use other's English translation.

5) Today I have no time to discuss the relation of his changing view of history and his personal life. *An Historian's Conscience: The Correspondence of Arnold Toynbee and Columba Cary-Elwes, Monk of Ampleforth* (Beacon Press, 1986) edited by Christian B. Peper, and William H. McNeill, *Arnold J. Toynbee: A Life* (Oxford University Press, 1989) reveal the connection. As far as I know, the correlation between his changing view of history and his personal life has not been fully discussed so far. In order to understand him and his view of history holistically, this research is indispensable.

6) M. F. Ashley Montagu, ed., *Toynbee and History: Critical Essays and Reviews* (Porter Sargent Publisher: Boston, 1956), p. 372.

7) See also *A Study of History, Illustrated*. Chapter 53 "The nature of historical thought," pp. 48–488.

8) See my paper, "Toynbee's View of Religion in an Age of Ecumenism," on June 15, 1995 at the 24th Conference of ISCSC at Wright State University, Dayton, Ohio.

Section 2   Toynbee's View of Religion in a Multi-Religious World

*   The main of this paper was presented on June 15, 1995 at Wright State University, Dayton, Ohio, U.S.A. for the 24th Annual Meeting of the International Society for the Comparative Study of Civilizations.

1) a) *Foreign Affairs*, Summer 1993, pp. 22–49. Though the main body of this article is disputable, the last sentence is, I think, convincing: "For the relevant future, there will be no universal civilization, but instead a world of different civilizations, each of which will have to learn to coexist with the others."

b) *The Clash of Civilizations and the Remaking of World Order* (New York: Simon & Schuster, 1996). We have to pay more attention to the latter half, i.e., *the Remaking of World Order* in order to avoid unnecessary misunderstandings.

2) We need to learn the wisdom of Matteo Ricci and Jesuit's policy. See *A Study of History*, Vol. VII, 441–442 and Sukehiro Hirakawa, *Matteo Ricci I* (Toyo Bunko, No. 141).
3) *The Works of Nathaniel Hawthorne* (Ohio State University Press, 1974), Vol. XI, pp. 161–169.
4) *Ibid.*, 163.
5) *Ibid.*, 165.
6) *Ibid.*, 166.
7) Aristotle, *The Poetics* (Loeb Classical Library, No. 199: 1927, 1973), p. 35.
8) Father Columba Cary-Elwes's letter to Mr. Christian B. Peper dated June 15, 1993, p. 2.
9) Arnold J. Toynbee, *A Study of History* (Oxford University Press, 1954), Vol. VII, p. 428.
10) Toynbee, *A Study of History*, Vol. VII, pp. 716–736, "Higher Religions and Psychological Types."
11) Kenneth Winetrout, *After One Is Dead: Arnold Toynbee As Prophet* (Hillside Press, Hampden, MA., 1989), p. 42. See also the same author's *Arnold Toynbee: The Ecumenical Vision* (Twayne Publishers, Boston, 1975), p. 120.
12) *A Study of History*, VII, 428, footnote 2.
13) *Ibid.*, footnote 2, 428–429. See also Christian B. Peper, ed., *An Historian's Conscience: The Correspondence of Arnold J. Toynbee and Columba Cary-Elwes, Monk of Ampleforth* (Beacon Press, Boston, 1986), pp. 393–394, pp. 179–180, pp. 242, 292, 451.
14) Radhakrishnan, S., *Eastern Religions and Western Thought*, 2nd edition (Oxford University Press, 1940), pp. 347–8. Quoted in Toynbee, *A Study of History*, Vol. VII, 735–6.
15) A. J. Toynbee, *Aquaintances* (Oxford University Press, 1967), Preface, p. v.
16) Peper, p. 526.
17) Peper, p. 156.
18) Arnold Toynbee, *An Historian's Approach to Religion* (Oxford University Press, 2nd ed. 1979), p. vii.
19) *Ibid.*, p. vii.

Section 3   The Paths of Spiritual Transmission in Case of Jesus Christ, Gautama Buddha, and Kūkai

*   Prepared for presentation at the 35th Annual Meeting of the International Society for the Comparative Study of Civilizations at the Institut Nation d'historie de Art. INHA, Paris, France on July 6, 2006.

1)   Roman and Arabic numbers in parentheses in my text refer respectively to Arnold J. Toynbee, *A Study of History*, 12 vols. (Oxford University Press, 1934–61).

2)   Paul Carus, *The Gospel of Buddha: According to Old Records*, 5th ed. Chicago, The Open Court Publishing Company, 1897, p. 19.

3)   Fred Gladstone Bratton, *A Story of the Bible,* Boston: Beacon Press, 1959, p. 217.

4)   Wilber M. Smith, *Therefore, Stand,* Natick, Mass. W. A. Wilde, 1959, pp. 247–248.

5)   坂本幸男,岩本裕訳注『法華経』上・中・下,岩波文庫,1962, 1977.

Chapter III   Civilizations and Morals
Section 1   Legitimacy, the Line of Succession, and Polity

*   June 22, 1996 at California State Polytechnic University, Pomona, California for the 25th Annual Meeting of International Society for the Comparative Study of Civilizations

1)   Arnold J. Toynbee, *A Study of History, Illustrated* (Oxford University Press, 1972), p. 268.

2)   Robert N. Bellah, *The Broken Covenant: American Civil Religion in Time of Trial* (The University of Chicago Press, 1975, 2nd ed. 1992), pp. 164–188.

3)   *Ibid.*, xxii.

4)   *Ibid.*, p. x.

5)   Chikuro Hiroike, *A Treatise on Moral Science* [in Japanese] (The Institute of Moralogy, Chiba-ken, Japan, 1928), pp. 1685–86.

6)   Ralph Waldo Emerson, "Concord Hymn," line 4.

7) Bernard Bailyn, "The Origins and Character of the American Revolution: An Interpretation," read on September 5, 1975 at "Asia and Pacific Regional Conference of American Studies Specialists," Fujinomiya, Japan.
8) James Bryce, *The American Commonwealth*, 3rd ed. (New York: The Macmillan Co., 1907), Vol. I. Chap. viii. pp. 78–85.
9) Bryce, p. 71.
10) *Ibid.*
11) James G. Frazer, *The Golden Bough*, Part VII, *Balder the Beautiful* (London, Macmillan, 1913, 1963), I. 2. and also see II. 287. Part I, I, 8–9.
12) Reinhart Bendix, *Kings or People: Power and the Mandate to Rule* (University of California Press, 1978), p. 602.
13) *Ibid.*, p. 598.
14) Robert E. Ball, C. B., M. B. E., LL. B. *The Crown, The Sages and Supreme Morality* (Routledge & Kegan Paul, London, 1983) (During his writing of this book, I had the honor to assist him.)
15) Bellah, p. 165. See also p. 166.
16) The Institute of Moralogy, *An Outline of Moralogy: A New Approach to Moral Science* (Chiba-ken, Japan: The Institute of Moralogy, 1987), pp. 111–113.
17) Benjamin R. Barber, *An Aristocracy of Everyone: The Politics of Education and the Future of America* (New York: Ballantine Books, 1992), p. 5.
18) Quoted in Robert Bellah, *The Broken Covenant*, p. 187.

Section 2   Global Ethics in Practice

*   Presented at the 29th Annual Meeting of the International Society for the Comparative Study of Civilizations held at the University of South Alabama, Mobile, Alabama on June 8, 2000. The present paper was slightly modified.

1) a) Quincy Wright, *A Study of War*, 2 vols. Chicago, 1942.
   b) Matthew Melko, *Peace in Our Time* (New York: Paragon House, 1990), Chapter 4 "Peace and Violence in the World as a Whole," pp. 90–130.

c) Michael Murphy Andregg, *On the Causes of War*. St. Paul, Minnesota, Ground Zero Minnesota, 1996, revised 1997. A very detailed study.

2) Lawrence E. Harrison & Samule P. Huntington eds., *Culture Matters: How Values Shape Human Progress*. Basic Books, 2000, xxvi–xxvii.

    During and after the session, Dr. Michael Murphy Andregg gave me valuable suggestions concerning global ethics. He showed me "Introduction," and "The Principles of a Global Ethic" made by an Editorial Committee of the Council of the Parliament of the World's Religions in Chicago on the basis of the Declaration composed in Tübingen (here headed 'Principles'), read out publicly at the solemn concluding plenary on 4 September 1993 in Grant Park, Chicago. This was subscribed to by: Bahai, Brahma Kumaris, Buddhism, Christianity, Native religions, Hinduism, Jainism, Judaism, Islam, Neo-pagans, Sikhs, Taoists, Theosophists, Zoroastrians, Inter-religious organizations, etc. I am appreciative of his suggestions.

3) Edward Tivnan, *The Moral Imagination: Confronting the Ethical Issues of Our Day*. New York: Simon & Schuster, 1995, p. 8.
4) *Ibid.*, p. 30.
5) *Ibid.*, p. 47.
6) *Ibid.*, p. 47.
7) Robert N. Bellah, Richard Madsen, William M. Sullivan, Ann Swindler, Steven M. Tipton, *The Good Society*. New York: Alfred A. Knopf, 1992, p. 129.
8) The Mainichi Newspaper, May 7, 1970.
9) Nathaniel Hawthorne, *The Centenary Edition of the Works of Nathaniel Hawthorne*. Ohio State University Press, 1974, Vol. XI, pp. 275–277.
10) ———. Vol. X, p. 87.
11) Samuel P. Huntington, *The Clash of Civilizations and the Remaking of World Order*. New York: Simon & Schuster, 1996, p. 320.

12) Joseph Needham, *Science and Civilization in China*. Cambridge University Press, 1956, Vol. II, p. 35.
13) Lao Tsu, *Tao Te Ching*, A New Translation by Gia-Fu Feng and Jane English. Random House, New York, 1972. No pagination. Chapter one.
14) 阿部吉雄, 山本敏夫, 市川安司, 遠藤哲夫『老子荘子　上　新釈漢文大系』明治書院, 1966, 1989, pp. 11–12. My English translation.
15) 伊東俊太郎『自然』三省堂 (Shuntaro Ito, *Nature*. Sanseido), 1999.

Section 3　Toward Common Wisdom

* Prepared for presentation at the 35th Annual Meeting of the International Society for the Comparative Study of Civilizatios At the Institut Nation d'historie de Art. INHA, Paris, France on July 6, 2006.
1) SM, Roman and Arabic numbers in parentheses in my text refer respectively to *Towards Supreme Morality: An Attempt to Establish the New Science of Moralogy*, by Chikuro Hiroike, LL.D (Kashiwa-shi, Chiba-ken, Japan: The Institute of Moralogy, 2002), 4 vols., volume number, and page number. Its original Japanese title *Dotokukagaku no Ronbun*, literally, *A Treatise on Moral Science*.
2) Arnold J. Toynbee, *A Study of History*, 12 vols. (Oxford University Press, 1934–61), Vol. 7, p. 771.

———, *A Study of History, Illustrated* (Oxford University Press, 1972).
3) ———, *An Historian's Approach to Religion* (Oxford University Press, 1956, 2nd ed., 1979).
4) *Ibid.*, chapter 19, "The Task of Disengaging the Essence from the Non-essentials in Mankind's Religious Heritage," pp. 261–283.
5) *A Study of History*, Vol. 7, p. 429.
6) *A Study of History*, Vol. 7, pp. 428–429.
7) *An Historian's Conscience: The Correspondence of Arnold J. Toynbee and Columba Cary-Elwes, Monk of Ampleforth,*

edited by Christian B. Peper (Boston: Beacon Press, 1986).
8) William H. McNeill, *Arnold J. Toynbee: A Life* (Oxford University Press, 1989).
9) *A Study of History*, volume 7, pp. 425–444.
10) *A Study of History*, volume 7, pp. 442–443.
11) *A Study of History*, volume 7, pp. 448.
12) *A Study of History*, volume 7, pp. 428.
13) See my paper, "Civilizations and Morals: Legitimacy, the Line of Succession, and Polity" in *Journal for the Comparative Study of Civilizations*, No. 2, pp. 31–37. Kashiwa-shi, Chiba-ken Japan: Reitaku University. March 1997 and also "For the Internationalization of Moralogy—A Tentative Reply to Dr. Lauwerys' Proposals on National Ortholinon—" Its Japanese translation is 川窪啓資「モラロジーの国際化のために ― ラワリーズ博士の国家伝統に関する御提案に対する管見 ―」『モラロジー研究』No. 8, 1979年3月, pp. 103–143.
14) See Henry Adams, *The Education of Henry Adams* (New York: The Modern Library, 1918), vi. And (14).
15) Cf. Herman Melville, *Pierre, or The Ambiguities*, book XIV, iii, "Chronometricals and Horologicals," in The Library of America, 1984, Herman Melville, pp. 247–252.
16) Lawrence E. Harrison & Samuel P. Huntington, eds. *Culture Matters: How Values Shape Human Progress.* New York: Basic Books, 2000. pp. vvi–xxvii.
17) *A Study of History*, Vol. 7, p. 515.
18) *A Study of History*, Vol. 7, p. 522.

Chapter IV   Two Civilizations and One City
Section 3   A Glimpse of China: Past, Present, and Future
*   Prepared for presentation at the 36th Annual Meeting of the International Society for the Comparative Study of Civilizations at the Asilomar Conference Center, Pacific Grove (Monterey), California, U.S.A. on June 14, 2007.
1) *Shi Ji, Historical Records*, Vol. II, Chap. II, Xie Dynasty.
2) However it might be praised, it became the good excuse of later rebellions.

3) Paul Kennedy, *The Rise and Fall of the Great Powers: Economic Change and Military Conflict from 1500 to 2000*, New York, Random House, 1987, p. 4.
4) Paul Kennedy, *The Rise and Fall of the Great Powers: Economic Change and Military Conflict from 1500 to 2000*, pp. 6–7.
5) Paul Kennedy, p. 7. And also refer to
   a) Masakatsu Miyazaki, *Teiwa no Nankai Daiensei*, Tokyo, Chukoushinsho, 1997.
   b) Gavin Menzies, *1421 The Year China Discovered the World*. Tokyo, Sony Magazines, 2003.
   c) Louise E. Levathes, *When China Ruled the Sea: Treasure Fleet of Dragon Throne 1405–1433*, New York, Simon & Schuster, 1994.
6) Sukehiro Hirakawa, *Matteo Ricci: Life*, 3 vols, Heibonnsha, Tokyo, 1997. Chinese ethnocentrism, Sinocentrism, III, 22.
7) John K. Fairbank, Edwin O. Reischauer, Albert M. Craig, *East Asia Tradition and Transformation*, 1976, pp. 229–230.
8) *Survey of International Affairs, 1926,* 1928 published, p. 235.

Section 4 St. Petersburg Viewed from Comparative Civilizations

*   Presented at the 32nd Annual Meeting of the International Society for the Comparative Study of Civilizations held at St. Petersburg, Russia, on September 18, 2003.
1-a) John Channon and Robert Hudson, *The Penguin Historical Atlas of Russia*, 1995.
1-b) Reinhard Bendix, *Kings or People: Power and the Mandate to Rule* (University of California Press, Berkeley, 1978)
2)   Arnold Toynbee, *Civilization on Trial* (Oxford University Press, 1948), chapter 9 (A. Meridian Book, New American Library Press, 1976), p. 153.
3)   Toynbee, VIII, 321–322.
4)   Conrad Totman, "Tokugawa Japan," in *An Introduction to Japanese Civilization,* ed. by Arthur E. Tiedemann (New York: Columbia University Press, 1974), p. 122.

Notes to pages 112–124

5) Bendix, p. 494.
6) Thomas Garrigue Masaryk, *Rusko A Evropa*, tr. into Japanese by Tatsuo Ishikawa (Yokohama: Seibunsha, 2002).
7) Toynbee, VIII, 580.
8) Toynbee, VIII, 581.
9) Toynbee, VIII, 582.
10) Arnold J. Toynbee, assisted by V. M. Boulter, *Survey of International Affairs, 1930* (Oxford University Press, 1931), p. 187.
11) *Ibid.*, 187–188.
12) *Ibid.*, 187–188.
13) Pitirim Sorokin, *Altruistic Love: A Study of American "Good Neighbors" and Christian Saints* (Boston: The Beacon Press, 1950).
14) The Institute of Moralogy, *An Outline of Moralogy: A New Approach to Moral Science* (Kashiwa, Japan: The Institute of Moralogy, 1987), p. 66.
15) T. S. Eliot, *The Complete Poems and Plays 1909–1950* (New York: Harcourt, Blace & World), p. 48, II. 372–377.

Chapter V The Civilizational Soul
Section 1 Introducing Moralogy: Bridging the East and the West

* Presented at the 27th annual conference of the International Society for the Comparative Study of Civilizations at Reitaku University, Chiba-ken, Japan, on June 11, 1998.
1) The Institute of Moralogy, *Chikuro Hiroike: A Pictorial Biography* (The Institute of Moralogy, Chiba-ken, 1970), p. 17.
2) *Ibid.*, p. 19.
3) Keisuke Kawakubo, "Chikuro Hiroike and the West," in *Chikuro Hiroike and Moralogy*, edited and published by the Institute of Moralogy, Chiba-ken, Japan, 1989, pp. 471–514, especially pp. 496–499. The following bibliography on moral science may be interesting:
   1. 1780: Jeremy Bentham (1748–1832). *An Introduction to*

the Principles of Morals and Legislation.
2. 1780: Benjamin Franklin (1709–90)'s letter to Joseph Priestly on February 8, 1780.
3. 1790: James Beattie (1735–1803). *Elements of Moral Science*, Vol. I. (T. Cadell, London, and W. Creeck, Edinburgh, 1790).
4. 1792: Adam Ferguson (1723–1816). *Principles of Moral and Political Science, being chiefly a retrospect of lectures delivered in the college of Edinburgh*. Edinburgh, printed for A. Strahan and T. Cadell (etc.), 2 vols.
5. 1793: James Beattie. *Elements of Moral Science*, Vol. II. (T. Cadell, London, and W. Creeck, Edinburgh, 1793).
6. 1828: George Payne (1781–1848). *Elements of Mental and Moral Science.*
7. 1835: Francis Wayland (1796–1865). *The Elements of Moral Science.*
8. 1852: Archibald Alexander (1772–1851). *Outlines of Moral Science.* New York, C. Scribner.
9. 1853: Laurens Perseus Hickok (1798–1888). *A System of Moral Science.* New York, Schenectady.
10. 1860: John Leadley Dagg (1794–1884). *The Elements of Moral Science.* New York, Sheldon & Company.
11. 1860: Ralph Waldo Emerson (1803–1882). *The Conduct of Life*, chapter VI. (*The Complete Works*. vol. VI, pp. 240–241).
12. 1862: James Mackintosh (1765–1832). *Ethical Philosophy*, 1830. "The purpose of the Moral Sciences is to answer the question What ought to be?" (Introduction, l862).
13. 1867: Mark Hopkins (1802–1887). *Lectures on Moral Science.* Delivered before the Lowell Institute, Boston. Boston, Could and Lincoln; New York, Sheldon and Company.
14. 1874: Henry Sidgwick (1833–1900). *The Methods of Ethics.* 1st ed. 1874, 2nd ed. 1877, 7th ed. 1907, and reissued in 1962, London, Macmillan. Wayland's *Elements of Moral Science* is quoted on p. 256, note in the 1962 edition.

15. 1880: Laurens Perseus Hickok. *A System of Moral Science*. Revised with the cooperation of Julius H. Steelye. Boston & London, Ginn & Company, Publishers, 1880, 1899.
16. 1882: Leslie Stephen (1832–1904). *The Science of Ethics*. 1st ed. 1882, 2nd ed. 1907. London, Smith, Elder & Co.
17. 1885: Noah Porter (1811–1892). *The Elements of Moral Science: Theoretical and Practical*. New York, C. Scribner's Sons.
18. c. 1892: James Harris Fairchild (1817–1902). *Moral Science; or The Philosophy of Obligation*. Rev. ed. New York, American Book Company. (First published in 1869 under the title, *Moral Philosophy or, the Science of Obligation*).
19. 1916: W. E. Hamilton. *Studies in Moral Science*. Chicago, Donnelley.
20. 1918: Chikuro Hiroike began to use the term, "moral science."
21. 1926: Hiroike coined a new word, "Moralogy."
22. 1928: Hiroike. *A Treatise on Moral Science: The First Attempt at Establishing Moralogy as A New Science*. 『道徳科学の論文』
23. 1957: John A. Oesterle (b. 1912). *Ethics: the Introduction to Moral Science*. Englewood Cliffs, J. J., Prentice-Hall.
24. 1963: Francis Wayland. *The Elements of Moral Science*, ed. by Joseph L. Blau. The Belknap Press of Harvard University Press, Cambridge, Massachusetts. The original text of this edition is the 1837 edition. Cf. No. 7.
25. 1969: Kenneth E. Boulding (b. 1910). "Economics as a Moral Science" in *American Economics Review* (March, 1969), 1–12.
26. 1974: Abraham I. Melden (b. 1910). "Recent Tendencies in American Moral Philosophy." A lecture delivered at the Kyoto American Studies Summer Seminar on July 19, 1974. He says, "Moral science may be a branch of psychology, sociology, or whatever."
27. 1975: Pierre Teilhard de Chardin. *Toward the Future*, tr. by Rene Hague, Collins, London. pp. 130–33.

4) Francis Wayland, *The Elements of Moral Science*, ed. by Joseph L. Blau (The Belknap Press of Harvard University Press, 1963), p. 5.
5) *Ibid.*, p. xliii.
6) *Ibid.*, p. xxvii.
7) Leslie Stephen, *The Science of Ethics*, Chapter 1, Section ii.
8) See Chikuro Hiroike, *A Treatise on Moral Science*, Chapter 1, Section 5, "Sciences on which the system of Moralogy is based."
9) Chikuro Hiroike, *The Characteristics of Moralogy and Supreme Morality*, tr. by the Institute of Moralogy, 1942, 1976, p. 154. A recent textbook is *An Outline of Moralogy: A New Approach to Moral Science* (The Institute of Moralogy, 1987, 1991).
10) See Arnold Toynbee, *An Historian's Approach to Religion* (Oxford University Press, 1979), p. 262.
11) *Ibid.*, Chap. 19, "The Task of Disengaging the Essence from the Non-essentials in Mankind's Religious Heritage," pp. 261–283.
12) 1 Corinthians 13: 12.
13) Jawaharlal Nehru, *The Discovery of India* (Delhi, Oxford University Press, 1946, 1989), p. 130. See also Radhakrishnan, *Indian Philosophy*, Vol. I, p. 466.
14) Hiroike, *The Characteristics*, p. 233.
15) See Pitirim Sorokin, *Social & Cultural Dynamics: A Study of Change in Major Systems of Art, Truth, Ethics, Law, and Social Relationships.*, Revised and abridged in one volume by the author, With a New Introduction by Michel P. Richard (Transaction Publishers, 1985, 1991), pp. 414–418.
16) Samuel P. Huntington, *The Clash of Civilizations and the Remaking of World Order* (Simon & Schuster, New York: 1996), p. 320.
17) The first chapter of *The Great Learning*.

Section 2 For the Internationalization of Moralogy
1) Arnold J. Toynbee, *An Historian's Approach to Religion*

2) (Oxford University Press, 1956). The page numbers in my text refer to this book.
2) Chikuro Hiroike, *Towards Supreme Morality*, Vol. III, p. 118.
3) *Towards Supreme Morality*, Vol. III, p. 133.
4) *Towards Supreme Morality*, Vol. III, pp. 131–132.
5) The Imperial Constitution of the Great Japan, (1889), Article 4.
6) The Constitution of Japan, (1946), Article 1.
7) *Towards Supreme Morality*, Vol. III, p. 133.
8) Toynbee, *A Study of History* (Oxford Univ. Press, 1934, 1963), III, 362.
9) Henry Adams, *The Education of Henry Adams* (New York, The Modern Library, 1918), vi.
10) Henry Adams, p. 16.
11) *Towards Supreme Morality*, Vol. III, p. 135.
12) Max Lerner, *America as a Civilization* (New York, 1957), p. 467.
13) Alexis de Tocqueville, *Democracy in America* (New York, Vintage Books, 1835, 1945), I, 30.
14) James Bryce, *Modern Democracies* (London, Macmillan, 1921), I, 70.
15) Ralph Waldo Emerson, "Concord Hymn," line 4.
16) Bernard Bailyn, "The Origins and Character of the American Revolution; An Interpretation," read on September 5, 1975 at "Asia and Pacific Regional Conference of American Studies Specialists," Fujinomiya, Japan.
17) A Treatise, 4, 1046, 1050–56.
18) James Bryce, *The American Commonwealth*, 3rd ed. (New York, The Macmillan Co., 1907), Vol. I, chap. viii, pp. 78–85.
19) Bryce, p. 71.
20) Bryce, p. 71.
21) James G. Frazer, *The Golden Bough*, Part VII. *Bolder the Beautiful* (London, Macmillan, 1913, 1963), I. 2 and also see II. 287 Part I. I, 8–9.
22) Max Learner, p. 535.
23) *A Treatise*, p. 2351.
24) Henry Steele Commager, *Meet the U.S.A.* (New York, 1970),

Chap. 3.
25) Max Learner, p. 371.
26) *Towards Supreme Morality*, Vol. III, p. 177.
27) J. F. Kennedy, "Inaugural Address," 1961.

Section 3 Two Japanese Masters of the Civilizational Soul: Hiroike Chikuro and Mori Ōgai

1) a) Arnold J. Toynbee, *A Study of History* (Oxford University Press, 1934), Vol. I, pp. 271–299 and Vol. I, pp. 1–394.
b) Toynbee, *A Study of History, Illustrated* (Oxford University Press, 1972), Chap. 13, pp. 97–109.
2) a) Toynbee, *A Study of History*, Vol. VIII, pp. 88–732 and Vol. IX, pp. 1–166.
b) Toynbee, *A Study of History, Illustrated*, Chapters 44–52.
3) a) Toynbee, *A Study of History* (Oxford University Press, 1954), Vol. VIII, pp. 580–629.
b) Toynbee, *A Study of History, Illustrated*, pp. 436–442.
4) Philip Bagby, *Culture and History: Prolegomena to the Comparative Study of Civilizations* (University of California Press, 1958).
5) Yamamoto Shin, *Toynbee and the Issues of the Study of Civilizations* (Keifu Shobo, 1969), pp. 142–180.
6) a) Sato Seizaburo, *Beyond the "Deadly Jump—the Western Impact and Japan"* (Toshi Shuppan, 1992).
b) ———, "Response to the West: The Korean and Japanese Patterns," in *Japan: A Comparative View*, edited by Albert M. Craig (Princeton University Press, 1979), pp. 105–129.
c) Hirakawa Sukehiro, *The Western Impact and Japan* (Kodansha Gakujutsu Bunko, 1985).
d) ———, *Wakon Yōsai no Keifu* (Kawade shobo, 1971).
7) a) Richard John Bowring, *Mori Ōgai and the Modernization of Japanese Culture* (Cambridge University Press, 1979), p. 19.
b) Kobori Keiichiro, *Mori Ōgai in his Young Days* (Tokyo University Press, 1969), pp. 185–293.
c) *Allgemeine Zeitung*, Nos. 175 and 178, June 26 and 29, 1886.

8) The Institute of Moralogy, *An Outline of Moralogy: A New Approach to Moral Science* (Kashiwa, Chiba-ken, Japan: The Institute of Moralogy, 1987), p. 5.
9) Hiroike Chikuro, *The Characteristic of Moralogy and Supreme Morality*, New Revised Edition (The Institute of Moralogy, 1996), p. 3.
10) a) "The Newsletter of the Institute of Moralogy," Vol. 10, No. 5, pp. 11–12. August, 1965.
    b) Kawakubo Keisuke, "Hiroike Chikuro and the West" in *Hiroike Chikuro and Moralogy* (The Institute of Moralogy, Chiba-ken, Japan, 1989), pp. 471–514.
11) President Roger Williams Wescott recommends me to read Julian Jaynes, *The Origin of Consciousness in the Breakdown of the Bicameral Mind* (Boston: Houghton Mifflin Company, 1976, 1990).

Section 4 The Unprecedentedness of Moralogy Viewed from the History of Western Moral Science
References

Adams, Henry. *Mont-Saint-Michel and Chartres: A Study of the Thirteenth-Century Unity*, 1904, 1913.

———. *The Education of Henry Adams: A Study of Twentieth-Century Multiplicity*, 1907, 1918.

Barber, Benjamin R. *An Aristocracy of Everyone: The Politics of Education and the Future of America* (New York, Ballantine Books, 1992).

Beattie, James (1735-1803). *Elements of Moral Science*, vol. I, 1790, vol. II, 1793 (Philadelphia, Press of Mathew Crey, 1790-1793).

Bentham, Jeremy (1748-1832). *An Introduction to the Principles of Morals and Legislation*, 1789.

Eliot, Thomas Stearns. *The Waste Land: A Facsimile and Transcript of the Original Drafts Including the Annotations of Ezra Pound*, Edited and written an Introduction by Valerie Eliot (A Harvest Special, New York, 1971).

Emerson, Ralph Waldo (1803-1882). He used "moral science" in *The Conduct of Life*, Chapter VI (The Complete Works, vol. VI, pp.

240-241).

Fairbank, John K., Edwin O. Reischauer, Albert M. Craig. *East Asia, Tradition and Transformation*, Herbert University, 1973, Houghton Mifflin.

Ferguson, Adam (1723-1816). *Principles of Moral and Political Science*, 2 vols. 1792, Edinburgh.

Franklin, Benjamin. His letter to Joseph Priestley on February 8, 1780.

Handlin, Oscar. *The Uprooted*. New York (1951).

Hiroike, Chikuro. *The Works of Hiroike*, LL.D. 4 vols.
- Vol. I   a. *The History of "Nakatsu"*
  - b. *An Unauthorized History of Japanese Imperial Family*
  - c. *A Study of TE-NI-WO-HA: A Chapter on Japanese Grammar*
- Vol. II   *An Outline of Chinese Grammar*, pp. 896.
- Vol. III   a. *An Introduction to Far Eastern Law*
  - b. *An Outline of Chinese Law*
- Vol. IV   a. *Isejingu, the Ancestral Shrine of the Japanese Emperors and the Fundamental Characters of Japan*
  - b. *The Origin of the Japanese Constitution*
  - c. *Suggestions to Capitalists, Directors, Managers, and Governmental Officials*

———. *Towards Supreme Morality: An Attempt to Establish the New Science of Moralogy*. The English Translation by the Institute of Moralogy, 4 vols. 2002.

Kawakubo, Keisuke. *From Toynbee to Comparative Study of Civilizations*. Nihon Hyouronsha, 2000 (in Japanese, 646 pages).

Payne, G. *Elements of Mental and Moral Science*, 1828: the first appearance of 'moral science' in the OED).

Porter, Noah. *The Elements of Moral Science: Theoretical and Practical* (New York, C. Scribner's Sons, 1885).

Sidgwick, Henry (1838-1900). *The Methods of Ethics* (London, 7th ed. 1962), His *The Methods of Ethics* (1st, 1874, 7th ed. 1901) is still good to refer.

Spengler, Oswald. *Der Untergang des Abendlandes* (1918-22).

Stephen, Leslie. *The Science of Ethics* (1882).

Tocqueville, Alexis de. *Democracy in America* (Henry Reeve text a

revised by Francis Bowen, 2 vols. New York: Vintage Books, 1945).
Twain, Mark. *The Adventure of Huckleberry Finn* (1884).
Wayland, Francis (1796-1865). *The Elements of Moral Science* (1st ed. 1835) edited with a detailed introduction by Joseph L. Blau, and was published from Harvard Univ. Press in 1963.

Bibliography

Adams, Henry. *The Education of Henry Adams: A Study of Twentieth-Century Multiplicity.* 1907, 1918.
———. *Mont-Saint-Michel and Chartres: A Study of the Thirteenth-Century Unity.* 1904, 1913.
Barber, Benjamin R. *An Aristocracy of Everyone: The Politics of Education and the Future of America.* New York, Ballantine Books, 1992.
Beattie, James (1735–1803). *Elements of Moral Science,* Vol. I, 1790, vol. II, 1793. Philadelphia, Press of Mathew Crey, 1790–1793.
Bendix, Reinhard. *Kings or People: Power and the Mandate to Rule.* University of California Press, Berkeley, 1978.
Bentham, Jeremy (1748–1832). *An Introduction to the Principles of Morals and Legislation,* 1789.
Bercovitch, Sacvan. *The Puritan Origins of the American Self.* Yale University Press, 1975.
———. ed., *The American Puritan Imagination: Essays in Evaluation.* Cambridge University Press, 1974.
Bergson, H.: *Les Deux Sources de la morale et de la Religion* (Paris 1932, Alcan).
Bibby, Reginald W. *Mosaic Madness: Pluralism Without A Cause.* Toronto, Canada, Stoddart, 1990, 1994.
Blaha, Stephen. *The Life Cycle of Civilizations.* Auburn, NH, Pingree-Hill Publishing, 2001–2002.

———. *A Unified Quantitative Theory of Civilizations and Societies, 9600 BC–2100 AD*. Auburn, NH, Pingree-Hill Publishing, 2005–6.
Boulding, Kenneth E. "Economics as a Moral Science." March, 1969.
Bratton, Fred Gladstone. *A Story of the Bible*. Boston: Beacon Press, 1959.
Carus, Paul. *The Gospel of Buddha: According to Old Records*, 5th ed. Chicago: The Open Court Publishing Company, 1897.
Channon, John and Robert Hudson. *The Penguin Historical Atlas of Russia*. 1995.
Confucius. *The Analects of Confucius*.
Daito-Shuppansha, ed., *Japanese-English Buddhist Dictionary*. 1965.
Eliot, T. S. *The Complete Poems and Plays 1909–1950*. New York: Harcourt, Blace & World.
———. *The Waste Land: A Facsimile and Transcript of the Original Drafts including the Annotations of Ezra Pound*, ed. by Valerie Eliot. New York, 1971.
Emerson, Ralph Waldo (1803–1882). He used "moral science" in *The Conduct of Life*, Chapter VI (The Complete Works, Vol. VI, pp. 240–241).
Fairbank, John K., Edwin O. Reischauer, Albert M. Craig. *East Asia Tradition and Transformation*. 1976.
Fairbank, John K., Edwin O. Reischauer, Albert M. Craig. *East Asia, Tradition and Transformation*. Herbert University, 1973, Houghton Mifflin.
Faulkner, William. *Light in August*. Penguin Modern Classics.
Ferguson, Adam (1723–1816). *Principles of Moral and Political Science*, 2 vols. 1792, Edinburgh.
Franklin, Benjamin. His letter to Joseph Priestley on February 8, 1780.
Frazer, James George. *The Golden Bough* (London, Macmillan, 1913, 1963), 13 vols.
Fuchs, Lawrence H. *The American Kaleidoscope: Race, Ethnicity and the Civic Culture*. Hanover and London, Wesleyan University Press, 1995.
Handlin, Oscar. *The Uprooted*. New York, 1951.
Hawthorne, Nathaniel. *The Works of Nathaniel Hawthorne*, Centenary Edition. Ohio State University Press, Vol. 1. *The Scarlet Letter*.

Hirakawa, Sukehiro. *Matteo Ricci: Life*, 3 vols. Heibonnsha, Tokyo, 1997. Chinese Ethnocentrism, Sinocentrism, III, 22.
Hiroike, Chikuro. *The Works of Hiroike, LL.D.* 4 vols.
Vol.I   a. *The History of "Nakatsu"*
       b. *An Unauthorized History of Japanese Imperial Family*
       c. *A Study of TE-NI-WO-HA: A Chapter on Japanese Grammar*
Vol.II   *An Outline of Chinese Grammar*, pp. 896.
Vol.III   a. *An Introduction to Far Eastern Law*
       b. *An Outline of Chinese Law*
Vol.IV   a. *Isejingu, the Ancestral Shrine of the Japanese Emperors and the Fundamental Characters of Japan*
       b. *The Origin of the Japanese Constitution*
       c. *Suggestions to Capitalists, Directors, Managers, and Governmental Officials*

———. *Towards Supreme Morality: An Attempt to Establish the New Science of Moralogy*. Translated into English by The Institute of Moralogy, Kashiwa-shi, Chiba-ken, Japan, 2002, 4 vols. Its original Japanese title is *Dōtokukagaku no Ronbun*, 1928, literally, *A Treatise on Moral Science*.

Huntington, Samuel P. *Who Are We?* The Challenges to America's National Identity. New York, Simon & Schuster, 2004.

Kawakubo, Keisuke. *From Toynbee to Comparative Study of Civilizations*. Nihon Hyouronsha, 2000 (in Japanese, 646 pages).

1)———. "Introducing Moralogy: Bridging the East and the West," in *Journal for the Comparative Study of Civilizations*, No. 4, pp. 91–99. Kashiwa-shi, Chiba-ken, Japan: Reitaku University. March 1999.

2)———. "Civilization and Religion in Toynbee," in *Journal for the Comparative Study of Civilizations*, No. 3, pp. 41–48. Kashiwa-shi, Chiba-ken, Japan: Reitaku University. March 1998.

3)———. "Civilizations and Morals: Legitimacy, the Line of Succession, and Polity," in *Journal for the Comparative Study of Civilizations*, No. 2, pp. 31–37. Kashiwa-shi, Chiba-ken, Japan: Reitaku University. March 1997. ("Civilizations and Morals: Legitimacy, the Line of Succession, and Polity" June 22, 1996 at

California State Polytechnic University, 25th Annual Meeting of ISCSC).
4)―――. "Global Ethics in Practice," in *Journal for the Comparative Study of Civilizations*, No. 6, pp. 47–53. Kashiwa-shi, Chiba-ken, Japan: Reitaku University. March 2001, 47–53.
5)―――. "Toynbee's View of Religion in a Multi-Religious World," in *Journal for the Comparative Study of Civilizations*, No. 7, pp. 11–18. Kashiwa-shi, Chiba-ken Japan: Reitaku University, March 2002.
6) 川窪啓資「高等宗教の比較的考察―アーノルド・J. トインビーと広池千九郎の求めたもの」『比較文明研究』第1号, 1996年3月発行, pp. 55–81.
7) Kawakubo, Keisuke. "For the Internationalization of Moralogy—A Tentative Reply to Dr. Lauwerys' Proposals on National Ortholinon―." Its Japanese translation is 川窪啓資「モラロジーの国際化のために ― ラワリーズ博士の国家伝統に関する御提案に対する管見 ―」『モラロジー研究』No. 8, 1979年3月, pp. 103–143.
8) 川窪啓資「広池千九郎と比較文明学」『比較文明研究』第7号, 2002年3月発行, pp. 119–132.
9)―――. "Hiroike Chikuro and Mori Ōgai as Cultural Initiators in Modern Japan," *Reitaku University Journal*, Vol. 59, December 1994, pp. 79–93.
Kennedy, John F. *A Nation of Immigrants*. Harper, 1964.
Kennedy, Paul. *The Rise and Fall of the Great Powers: Economic Change and Military Conflict from 1500 to 2000*. Random House, New York: 1987.
Lerner, Max. *America as a Civilization*, New York, Henry Holt, 1957, 30th Anniversary ed. 1987.
Levathes, Louise E. *When China Ruled the Sea: Treasure Fleet of Dragon Throne 1405–1433*. Simon & Schuster, New York, 1994.
Masaryk, Thomas. *Garrigue, Rusko A Evropa*. tr. into Japanese by Tsatsuo Ishikawa (Yokohama: Seibunsha, 2002). (1913) *Russland und Europa* ("Russia and Europe"). Jena, Germany. (English translation by Eden and *The Spirit of Russia*, London, 1919), *The Spirit of Russia* (tr., 2nd ed. 1955).

Mather, Cotton. *Magnalia Christi Americana*, Books I and II, ed. by Kenneth B. Murdock. The Belknap Press of Harvard University, 1977.
McNeill, William H. *Arnold J. Toynbee: A Life*. Oxford University Press, 1989.
Melville, Herman. *Pierre, or The Ambiguities*, book XIV, iii, "Chronometricals and Horologicals," in The Library of America, 1984, Herman Melville, pp. 247–252.
———. *Redburn*.
Menzies, Gavin. *1421 The Year China Discovered the World*. Sony Magazines, 2003, Tokyo.
Miyazaki, Akatsu. Teiwa no Nankai Daiensei, Chuukoushinsho, Tokyo, 1997.
Newberry, Frederick. *Hawthorne's Divided Loyalties: England and America in His Works*. London, 1987.
Payne, G. *Elements of Mental and Moral Science*, 1828: the first appearance of 'moral science' in the *OED*.
Porter, Noah. *The Elements of Moral Science: Theoretical and Practical*. New York, C. Scribner's Sons, 1885.
Pound, Ezra. *The Cantos of Ezra Pound*. A New Directions Book 1934, 1972.
Sakamoto, Yukio and Iwamoto, Yutaka (坂本幸男, 岩本裕訳注『法華経』上・中・下, 岩波文庫, 1962, 1977) trans. Saddharma pundarika-sutra. ed. by H. Kern and B. Nanjio, St. Petersbourg, 1912 (Bibliotheca Buddhica X).
Schlesinger, Jr. *The Disuniting of America: Reflections on a Multicultural Society*. New York, Norton, 1992.
Shang Shu (『尚書』) or *Shujing* (『書経』), *The book of Shang*, The Announcement of Zhong Hui.
Shiren (師錬), Kokan (虎関) (1278–1346). *Genkoushakusho* 『元亨釈書』, 30 vols. (鎌倉時代の禅僧が著した日本仏教史)
Sidgwick, Henry (1838–1900). *The Methods of Ethics* (London, 7th ed. 1962).
司馬談 (Sima Tan) and his son Sima Qian (司馬遷), *Shi Ji* (『史記』), *Historical Records*, Vol. II, Chap. II, Xie Dynasty (夏王朝).
Smith, Wilber M. *Therefore, Stand*. Natick, Mass. W. A. Wilde, 1959.

Sorokin, Pitirim. *Altruistic Love: A Study of American "Good Neighbors" and Christian Saints*. Boston: The Beacon Press, 1950.

Spengler, Oswald. *Der Untergang des Abendlandes* (1918–22), Verlag C.H.Beck Munchen 1923.

Stephen, Leslie. *The Science of Ethics* (1882).

The Institute of Moralogy, *An Outline of Moralogy: A New Approach to Moral Science*. Kashiwa, Japan: The Institute of Moralogy, 1987.

Tocqueville, Alexis de. *Democracy in America* (Henry Reeve text revised by Francis Bowen, 2 vols. New York: Vintage Books, 1945).

Totman, Conrad, "Tokugawa Japan," in *An Introduction to Japanese Civilization*, ed. by Arthur E. Tiedemann (New York: Columbia University Press, 1974).

Toynbee, Arnold J. *A Study of History*, 12 vols. Oxford University Press, 1934–61.

———. *A Study of History, Illustrated*. Oxford University Press, 1972.

———. *An Historian's Approach to Religion*. Oxford University Press, 1956, 2nd ed. 1979.

An Historian's Conscience: The Correspondence of Arnold J. Toynbee and Columba Cary-Elwes, Monk of Ampleforth, edited by Christian B. Peper. Boston: Beacon Press, 1986.

Toynbee, Arnold J. assisted by V. M. Boulter, *Survey of International Affairs, 1930*. Oxford.

Toynbee, Arnold. *Civilization on Trial* (Oxford University Press, 1948), chapter 9. (A. Meridian Book, New American Library Press, 1976), p. 153.

———. *Survey of International Affairs, 1926* (p. 235), (1928 published).

Twain, Mark. *The Adventure of Huckleberry Finn* (1884).

Wayland, Francis (1796–1865). *The Elements of Moral Science* (1st ed. 1835), edited with a detailed introduction by Joseph L. Blau, and was published from Harvard Univ. Press in 1963.

Winetrout, Kenneth, *After One Is Dead, Arnold Toynbee As Prophet: Essays in Honor of Toynbee's Centennial*, Hillrise Press, Hampton,

Massachusetts, U.S.A. 1989.

Index

abortion
 –the laws of 58
 –An elderly director of obstetrics in an abortion clinic in Tokyo 59
 –aborted children 60
Adams, Henry 147, 185
 –Adams, John-Adams, John Quincy-Adams, Charles Francis 147
Alexis 111
Amaterasu Ōmikami 70, 84–89, 157, 180–181, 183
Ambrose, St. 29, 68
America
 –"An Enormous Laboratory" of Mankind 91–100
 –American history 94
 –Pilgrim Fathers, The 46, 93–94
 –A Nation of Immigrants 95–98
 –American Democracy 148
 –The American War of Independence 149
Ānanda 37, 129
Antony, St. 116
Aristotle, *Poetics* 27
Asoka, King 37
Augustine, Saint, *De Civitate Dei* or *Civitas Dei* 18–20
Aum Shinrikyou 23

Bagby, Philip 5, 158
 –*Culture and History* 156
Bailyn, Bernard 48, 149
Ball, Robert E., *The Crown, the Sages and Supreme Morality* 50
Barber, Benjamin R. 52, 185
Beattie, James, *Elements of Moral Science* 122, 170–171
Bellah, Robert N., *The Broken Covenant* 45–46
 –*The Good Society* 58
Bentham, Jeremy, *An Introduction to the Principles of Morals and Legislation* 170
Bercovitch, Sacvan 92
Bergson, Henri, *Les Deux Sources de la morale et de la Religion* 36
Blaha, Stephen, *A Unified Quantitative Theory of Civilizations and Societies, 9600 B.C.-2100 A.D.* 97–98
Blau, Joseph L. 125, 172
Bradford, William, *Of Plymouth Plantation* 93
Bradley, Sculley, eds., *The American Tradition in Literature* 95
Bratton, Fred Gladstone 37
Bryce, James 49, 149–150
Byzantine civilization 111, 113

Callahan, Sydney & Daniel 57
Carus, Paul 36
Catherine II, Empress 117
Chaotic Society 49–50
Childe, Gordon V. 7
China 101–108
 –Three manners of Succession of the Throne in Ancient China, The 46
 –the Rule of Virtue (帝道) - the Rule of Right (王道) - the Rule of Might (霸道) 46
 –Announcement of Zhong Hui 46–47

–Tang of the Yin Dynasty 48
–Wu of the Zhou Dynasty 48
–Si Ma Qian 101
–Yao 101
–Shun 101
–*Shang Shu, The book of Shang* 102
–Chinese Dynasties 103
–Chinese Traditional View of their Surrounding Barbarians 104–105
–Ch'ing Dynasty 106
–Kang-xi-di 106
–*K'ang-hsi-Dictionary* 106
–Qian-long-di 106
–Kao-cheng-hsueh 106–107
–Ke-ju 107
Civilizational Disintegration 42
Civilizational Soul, The iv, 119, 122
Clinton, President 50
Columba, Father 31
Comparative Study of Civilizations, The Vistas of the 1
Confucius 47–48, 70, 73–77, 101, 122, 149, 183–184
–*Confucian Analects* 99, 107, 178, 183
Crèvecoeur, St. Jean de, *Letters from an American Farmer* 95
Croly, Raymond, *The Promise of American Life* 52

Daijousai (the Great Thanksgiving Festival) 86
Daniel the Stylite, Saint 116
Danilevskii, Nikolai 116
Dante 60
Da-tang, xi-yuji 40
Democracy 48–49
Descartes 62
Deshima 113
Dialogue between ISCSC and JSCSC 5
Dostoyevsky, Pyodor 116

Ecumenism 27
El Dorado 92
Eliot, T. S. 8, 94, 99
–*The Waste Land* 99–100, 117, 176
Emerson, Ralph Waldo 94, 133, 175
Encyclopedia Britannica 106
Esoteric Buddhism 8, 40–41
Essays in Chronological Order, The v–vi
European virus 99

Faulkner, William, *Light in August* 97
Frank, Andre Gunder 5
Frazer, James G. 17
–*The Golden Bough* 49, 150
Fukuzawa, Yukichi 4, 172

Geyl, Pieter 22
Glendon, Mary Ann 58
Global Ethics 55–63
Gray, Thomas, "Elegy Written in a Country Churchyard" 33–34
Greek Orthodox 110
Gutenberg 37

Harrison 56, 77
Hawthorne, Nathaniel
–"The Man of Adamant" 26
–"Alice Doane's Appeal" 59
–"Young Goodman Brown" 59–60
–*The Marble Faun* 86
–*The House of the Seven Gables* 87
–*The Scarlet Letter* 93
–*The English Notebooks,* and *Our Old Home* 98
Hermitage, the 117
Hideyoshi 112
Hiroike, Chikuro 162
–Supreme Morality 66, 70–77, 128, 164, 167

–*A Treatise on Moral Science* 70, 74–76, 78–79, 122, 124–125, 136, 164, 169
 –moralogy, The process in the making of 177–178
 –*A Treatise on Moral Science*, The Contents of 178–179
 –1. The application of modern sciences to the system of Moralogy 179–180
 –2. Hiroike's Methods 180–184
 –Moralogy iv, 123–133
 –*The Characteristics of Supreme Morality and Moralogy* 136
 –*Ise Jingu* 85
 –*Kojiruien* 123, 162, 177
 –five moral streams 164
 –the Institute of Moralogy 167
Hiroike, Mototaka 167
Hiroike Sentaro iv
Hobbes, Thomas, *Leviathan* 170
hubris 29, 68, 108
Huntington, Samuel P.
 –symbiosis of civilizations, the 11
 –*The Clash of Civilizations and the Remaking of World Order* 10, 25, 61, 65, 95, 130–132,
 –*Who Are We?* 96, 99

ISCSC: International Society for the Comparative Study of Civilizations iii, 5, 116
Ise Jingū or *Grand Shrine of Ise* 84, 177–178
 –*Sengu* 87–89
Islamic Afghanistan 114
island civilization, an 167
Ito, Shuntaro 4
 –*Nature* 62
Izanaginomikoto 84

James, Henry 94, 99
James, William 99

Japanese Civilization 83–89
 –Bibliography 89
Jaspers, Karl 63, 165
Jefferson 48–49
Jeffries, Vincent 9
Jesus Christ 71
Jinmu, 1st Emperor 86
Jitō, Empress 87, 89
Jiun Sonja 7–9
Jomon and *Yayoi* 83
Jung, Karl 28, 180

Kamikawa, Masahiko 5
Kaniṣka, King 37
Kawakubo, Keisuke iv, viii, 34
Kojiki 84
Kroeber, Alfred 4
Kūkai or Kōbō-Daishi 7, 40–42, 181
 –*Sangō Shīki* and *Himitsu Mandala Jūjūshinron* 7–8
Kumārajīva 40

Lao-tsu, *Lao-tsu's Morality Sutra* 61–62
Lauwerys 135–153
 –His proposals on National Ortholinon 146, 151
Legitimacy, the Line of Succession, and Polity 45–53
Lerner, Max 148, 151

Macartney, Lord 108
Mahākāśyapa 37
Mahāvairocana 41
Maitreya Bodhisattva 8
Masaryk, Thomas Garrigue, *Spirit of Russia, The* 113
Matteo Ricci 105–106
Mcilwaine, C. H. in *The Cambridge Medieval History* 146
McNeill, H. William 4–5
 –*Arnold J. Toynbee: A Life* 31, 69
Melko, Matthew 4, 83

Melville, Herman, *Moby-Dick* and *Redburn* 3
Mencius 48
Mission-oriented science, a 12
Monarchy 50
Montesquieu 52
Moralogy, the future of, What should be done for 184–185
Mori, Ōgai 122, 155–167
 –*Shibue Chūsai, Isawa Ranken* and *Hōjō Katei* 159
 –Ōgai's translation of Goethe's *Faust* 159
 –"Hebi" 161
 –Yasui fujin 162
 –a Herodian 167
Moscow, Church of 110
Moses 93

Nadia of Afghanistan 114–115
Naumann, Edmund 160
Needham, Joseph 61
Novgorod 109

Ortholinons
 –Family, National and Spiritual 51, 71
 –Quasi-Ortholinons 52
 –national ortholinon, three kinds of 142
 –National Ortholinon in the United Kingdom 145–146
 –National Ortholinon in the United States 147

Palencia-Roth, Michael 4–5
Paul, St. 38–39, 78, 129, 153
Payne, G., *Elements of Mental and Moral Science* 169–170
Peripheral civilization 115–116, 156–157
Perry, Commodore 158
Petersburg, St. 109–117

Peter the Great 109, 113, 115–116
Porter, Noah, *The Elements of Moral Science: Theoretical and Practical* 175–176
Pound, Ezra 8, 94, 99
Primary Chronicle, The 109
Pushkin, Aleksandr 116

Quigley 4

Rousseau 53
Rurik 110
Russia 109–113
Russian Orthodoxy 110

Saddharmapuṇḍarīka-sūtra 40, 79
Śākyamuni 72–73
 –*Shibunritsu (Si Fen Lu or The Vinaya [Rules of Discipline] in Four Divisions)* 72
Sanderson, ed., *Civilizations and World Systems* 4
San Felipe, the 112
Santayana, George 52
Satanic sciences of the West, the 115
Shimabara Peninsula, the massive rebellion on 112
Socrates 70–71, 184
Sorokin, Pitirim 4, 6, 9, 116
 –*Altruistic Love* 116
Spengler, Oswald, *Der Untergang des Abendlandes* 176
Spiritual Transmission in Case of Jesus Christ, Gautama Buddha, and Kūkai 35–42
Stephen, Leslie, *The Science of Ethics* 76, 125, 173–176
Sugawara Michizane 157
Susanoonomikoto 85
Symmachus, Quintus Aurelius 29, 68

Targowski, Andrew iii

Tenrikyo   124, 177
Textual or Lower Criticism   38
Theodosius   18
Tivnan, Edward   56–57
Tocqueville, Alexis de   148, 184
Tokugawa Bakufu   112
Tolstoy, Leo   116
Toynbee, Arnold J.   iii, 4
–metahistory   10
–The Historian's Angle of Vision   10
–An Illustrative Tree of Toynbee's Spiritual Life History (1889–1975)   32
–Lawrence and his wife Jean   33
–higher religion   15–21, 27, 66–69, 136, 165
–Churches as Cancers   17–18
–Churches as chrysalises   18–19
–Churches as a higher species of societies   19–20
–a higher species of society   19
–methodology and epistemology   21–23
–Religon in a Multi-Religious World   25–34
–*sub specie aeternitatis*   28
–Hinduism, Buddhism, Christianity, Islam   28–29
–Christian B. Peper, *An Historian's Conscience: The Correspondence of A. J. Toynbee and Columba Cary-Elwes, Monk of Ampleforth*   31, 69
–Religio Historici   33–34, 79
–*Survey of International Affairs, 1926*   107
–*Survey of International Affairs, 1931*   166
–Zealotism, Herodianism, Evangelism   113–116
–the founders of Higher Religions of the world; Amaterasu Ōmikami, Buddha, Confucius, Jesus Christ, Socrates, and some other Sages   122
–Challenge and Response   156
Translation   39–42
Tsukiyominomikoto   85
Tsutsumi, Takashi   7
Typology   92

Ultimate Spiritual Reality   33, 69
Umesao, Tadao   4
Universal Declaration of Human Rights   55

Vladimir   110

Washington, George   48–49, 149, 185
Wayland, Francis, *The Elements of Moral Science*   125, 171–173, 176
Wescott   4
Wilkinson, David   4–5
Winetrout   28
Winthrop, John   93, 98
Woolf, Virginia   174

Xi-you-ji   40
Xuan-Zang   40

Yamamoto, Shin   4, 157–158
Yasuda, Yoshinori   7
Young, Brigham   97

Keisuke Kawakubo
The Civilizational Soul

2015年5月31日　第1版第1刷発行
（定価は表紙カバーに表示してあります）

著　者　川　窪　啓　資

発行者　野　澤　幸　弘
発行所　株式会社行人社
〒162-0041 東京都新宿区早稲田鶴巻町537
電話 03(3208)1166　FAX 03(3208)1158　振替 00150-1-43093

ISBN 978-4-905978-90-9　C 3095　　　　　印刷　シナノ